ESSAYS ON ANCIENT FICTION

ESSAYS ON ANCIENT FICTION

BY

ELIZABETH HAZELTON HAIGHT

Professor of Latin, Vassar College

Essay Index Reprint Series

BOOKS FOR LIBRARIES PRESS, INC.

FREEPORT, NEW YORK

First published 1936
Reprinted 1966

To

FLORENCE GILMAN, M.D.

πολλῶν δ' ἀνθρώπων ἴδεν ἄστεα καὶ νόον ἔγνω,

ἀρνύμενος ἥν τε ψυχὴν καὶ νόστον ἑταίρων.

PREFACE

THIS book "Essays in Ancient Fiction" was conceived in a belief that today when one favorite pastime of the world is the reading of novels there ought to be a revival of interest in the two great Latin novels. Few even glance at the *Satyricon* and the *Metamorphoses* of Apuleius. Yet here are two racy, exciting stories full of ancient life and lore, color and flavor. Moreover, *The Loeb Classical Library* has made them easily available in excellent translations for those whose Latin is forgotten or who never had any.

So these essays aim to call attention to the *Satyricon* and the *Metamorphoses* and by giving some idea of their forerunners to set them in their proper place in the history of ancient fiction. The brilliant article on "The Greek Romances" by J. S. Phillimore [1] first showed me how necessary it was to study the precursors of the Latin novel as Phillimore had presented those of the Greek and to understand all the elements that went into its making. This book does not pretend to be a complete study of such material, for that could not be compassed in one volume. It should include both Greek and Latin forbears and the list is long.

Elements of Romance appeared among the Greeks in mythos and ainos, in epic poetry, in prose history especially in the logoi of Herodotus, in narrative speeches in tragedies and the romantic situations of Euripides' plays.

[1] In *English Literature and the Classics*, Oxford, 1912.

vii

Material for prose fiction was prepared in the New Attic Comedy, in Theophrastus' Characters, in the Alexandrian poetry of sentiment, in the Mimes of Herodas and Theocritus, in the Epyllion and in the Alexandrian epic of Apollonius Rhodius through his Medea story, in Parthenius' small *novelle*. In Latin literature too the art of narration was developed in prose in the *controversiae* of the rhetorical schools and in the *novelle* included in Livy's history. In poetry, the technique of story-telling reached a high point in Horace's Satires through his use of fable, fictitious interlocutor, dialogue and anecdote. And romance mounted to new emotional heights in Vergil's Aeneid with its tragic passion of Queen Dido and in elegiac poetry, formal and popular, with its new portrayal of intense personal emotion.

Much work has been done in presenting this wide field of ancient romance. And more is being done. Since Rohde's great work, *Die griechische Roman,* was written and revised, other significant studies have been published : Aly Wolf's *Volkmarchen, Sage und Novelle bei Herodot und seinen Zeitgenossen,* J. A. K. Thomson's *The Art of the Logos,* Marjorie Crump's *The Epyllion,* Norman De Witt's *The Romance of Queen Dido.* The phallic tradition as it descended through mimes and comedy old and new has been presented in various works concerned chiefly with origins and archaeology. My own book on *Romance in the Elegiac Poets* attempted to relate Parthenius and the Latin elegists to the development of ancient fiction.

In this present volume I do not propose to collate or summarize all this material or to produce any sequential history of ancient fiction. Rather I have aimed to write five separate essays which would secure the interest of the general reader for the field of ancient story-telling by

presenting to him new vistas and which might perhaps
extend for the student of Classics his knowledge of the
forerunners of the Latin novel and of the art of narration
in the *Satyricon* and the *Metamorphoses*.   In part this is
a source-book making available in one volume all sorts
of *novelle* in ancient literature which are seldom read.
In part it is a critical study of the art of narration among
the ancients particularly in the *Satyricon* and the *Metamorphoses* of Apuleius.   Because of the very nature of
the subject matter, I can affirm with confidence :

Lector, intende ; laetaberis.

It is a pleasure to make here several acknowledgments.
The quotations from volumes in the Loeb Classical
Library are made by the kind permission of the Presi-
dent and Fellows of Harvard College, the proprietors of
the Loeb Classical Library.   Grateful thanks are offered
to the Trustees of Vassar College for the leave of absence
which facilitated the completion of this book, to Presi-
dent Henry Noble MacCracken for his unfailing interest
in research and to the generous donors of the J. Leverett
Moore Research Fund in Classics which made possible
the publication of these essays.

CONTENTS

CONTENTS

ESSAYS ON ANCIENT FICTION

ESSAYS ON ANCIENT FICTION

I

ORIENTAL STORIES IN CLASSICAL PROSE LITERATURE

ANY student of ancient fiction is familiar with the eastern origin of much material in both Greek and Latin novels. The presence of these Oriental tales has given rise to various theories about the origin of ancient romance. An extreme statement of the debt to Orientalism is that of J. S. Phillimore in his essay on "The Greek Romances."

"The point has been disputed whether the Novel owes anything to influences definitely un-Greek. There is no room for doubt. . . The Novel is an import. . . Romance is something which arises always on the borders of Hellenism, and often derives its themes from over the border, e. g. a Cyrus and a Dido." [1]

This same point of view is expressed by S. Gaselee :

In fiction "we find one of the very few instances of the Greek mind under an external influence — it might almost be said Oriental ideas expressing themselves in Greek language and terms of thought.

"The most significant feature of the Greek novels is their un-Greek character. We can always point to Oriental elements in their substance, and almost always to Oriental blood in their writers." [2]

[1] J. S. Phillimore, "The Greek Romances," in *English Literature and the Classics*, Oxford, 1912, pp. 94–95.
[2] S. Gaselee, "Appendix on the Greek Novel," *Daphnis and Chloe*, in *The Loeb Classical Library*, p. 404.

Even in the early part of the nineteenth century when John Dunlop wrote his significant *History of Fiction,* various theories had been advanced about the origins of romance.   Dunlop refers to three special theories which he calls the Gothic, the Arabian (the Oriental) and the Classical systems, but he shows in a significant paragraph that he was aware that no one system can be pressed too far, especially the Oriental.

"A great number of those fables now considered as eastern, appear to have been originally Greek traditions, which were carried to Persia in the time of Alexander the Great, and were afterwards returned to Europe, with the modification they had received from oriental ideas." [3]

This hint of a possible eastern borrowing from Greece is developed fully and with considerable illustration by Erwin Rohde in a chapter of his epochal work, *Der griechische Roman.*[4]   Let me briefly paraphrase his line of thought.

The great epic poems of several ancient peoples probably go back to an original prehistoric common home. Yet they express in most individual ways the dreams and ideals of each people in their freshest creative period. Besides these peculiarly national epics, however, there exist in the literature and tradition of most people little stories in verse and prose which keep their identity in their wide wanderings.   They probably had their roots in vast Asia but their seeds blew all over the world and bore new blossoms.

These international tales can be traced in origin back to India.   They appear in Buddhist teaching in parables. There are literary collections of fables, *Märchen, Novelle,*

---

[3] John Dunlop, *The History of Fiction,* Philadelphia, 1842, vol. I. pp. 126–27.
[4] E. Rohde, *Der griechische Roman und seine Vorläufer,* Leipzig, 1914.   Anhang: "Uber griechische Novellendichtung und ihren Zusammenhang mit dem Orient," pp. 578–601.

arising under Buddhist influence such as Pantschatantra, the Parrot Book, the Sindabad Book, the twenty-five stories of the Vetâla.

These Indian stories wandered among the Persians, Syrians, Arabians and Jews, then farther on in the literature of the Latin language and the thought and tradition of European peoples. Treasures were exchanged in the contacts of East and West.

The search for the original sources of these stories leads back to India. But in the Indian collections of stories there appear certain *Märchen* and *Tierfabeln* which probably had their origin in Greece. The *Märchen* seem not to be the work of conscious, creative human genius, but rather a natural growth out of the life of early people. The animal stories are different. They do not have the naïve optimism and dream-like quality of the *Märchen* ; they are the result of an observant spirit viewing life coolly and ironically. Their peculiar habitat was certainly Greece, but they spread over East and West.

It is possible that the *Novelle* too which seem to have spread from the East (from India) to the West may have had their original home in Greece, migrated eastward and then returned westward from India. Certainly after the expeditions of Alexander the Great opportunity for such migration was abundant : many contacts of Seleucids with Indian kings, the travels of Onesicritus, Megasthenes and others to India, the close union of Greek and Indian culture (lasting 250–85 B.C.) in the Indian-Bactrian kingdom of the dynasty founded by Diodotus, the trade relations between India and Alexandria in Egypt.

It was natural that with the development of these *Novelle* there grew up in Greece, as there did in Arabia, in Italy, a special profession of public story-tellers. They were called *aretalogi* and their activities became very like

4 ESSAYS ON ANCIENT FICTION

those of the μῖμοι, ἠθολόγοι, θαυματοποιοί. Perhaps when after
Alexander the Great Greek culture flooded the Orient,
these Greek story-tellers went to the East. There is a
tradition of a collection of stories which Alexander had
told to himself during sleepless nights. Why might not
this be true ? The same thing was told of Augustus.[5]

Rohde illustrates his theory of the original Greek origin
of stories found in the East by the example of a story
written by Buddhagosha, a parable of Kisagotâmi (fifth
century). The same story appeared in Greek literature
at least one hundred years before Buddhagosha wrote
this parable. Julian tells it of Democritus and Darius [6]
and it appears in Lucian [7] and in the version of the History of Alexander by Pseudocallisthenes.[8] In this last
form the Greek story was imitated by many Oriental nations (Arabic, Hebrew, Persian). Finally it returned
to Europe and is one of the Novelle of Ser. Giovanni
Fiorentino, who wrote his Pecorone in 1378. The history of this story helps to confirm Rohde in his belief that
the Orient was indebted to the Greeks not only for the
animal fables, but also for many pearls of Novelle.

Perhaps the most significant fact that overtops all these
discussions of the origins of ancient fiction is that romance
was neither purely eastern nor western, but at its height
a result of fusion of Orient and Occident arising from
travel, trade and various other contacts, especially after
the time of Alexander the Great.

It is interesting to review the different kinds of eastern
stories referred to in ancient writers. Here surprisingly
Aristophanes is perhaps the first to give us rich and definite material. First we hear of gay stories told at dinner
parties, and very useful for averting wrath in difficult
situations if a man can only remember or invent some.

[5] Suet. 78.   [6] Letter 37.   [7] Demonax, 25.   [8] III. 23.

In *The Wasps,* a reproachful father, Philocleon, remarks to his son :

> No, no,
> Drinking ain't good : I know what comes of drinking,
> Breaking of doors, assault, and battery,
> And then, a headache and a fine to pay.

Bdelycleon, the son replies :

> Not if you drink with gentlemen, you know.
> They'll go to the injured man, and beg you off,
> Or you yourself will tell some merry tale,
> A jest from Sybaris, or one of Aesop's,
> Learned at the feast.   And so the matter turns
> Into a joke, and off he goes contented.[9]

Farther on in the play, Philocleon who has knocked over a Baking-Girl's basket of loaves, uses his son's advice, trying to soothe her wrath by a story.

Philocleon :
> A merry tale or two sets these things right.
> I'll soon set matters right with this young woman.

Baking-Girl :
> No, by the Twain ! you shan't escape scot-free,
> Doing such damage to the goods of Myrtia,
> Sostrata's daughter, and Anchylion's, Sir !

Philocleon :
> Listen, good woman : I am going to tell you
> A pleasant tale.

Baking-Girl :
> Not me, by Zeus, sir, no !

Philocleon :
> At Aesop, as he walked one eve from supper,
> There yapped an impudent and drunken bitch.
> Then Aesop answered, *O you bitch ! you bitch !*
> *If in the stead of that ungodly tongue*
> *You'd buy some wheat, methinks you'd have more sense.*[10]

It is hardly strange that the Baking-Girl declared that Philocleon was insulting her, for his story was not the

[9] *Vesp.* 1252–61. *Aristophanes,* translated by B. B. Rogers in *The Loeb Classical Library.* 3 vols. New York, 1930.
[10] *Ibid.,* 1401–5.

λόγον χαρίεντα or λόγος δεξιός which, in his drunken state, he labels it.

Two instances of the γέλοιον Συβαριτικόν are given in the same play, *The Wasps*, one of a woman of Sybaris, similar to the anecdote assigned by Aristophanes to Aesop,[11] the other about a man of Sybaris who, because he was a poor driver, fell out of a wagon and hurt his head only to be told by a friend standing by that the cobbler should stick to his last.[12]

If none of these Sybaritic jests seems to us very amusing or witty, at least we get an idea from them that such a tale was supposed to have a quick, pointed retort ; that they were so popular that wrath could be mollified by an apposite use of them ; and that such little sharp anecdotes as early as the fifth century B.C. had come to be attributed to Aesop or connected with the town of Sybaris in Magna Graecia.

Rohde points out that another type of special story connected with Sybaris seems to be one in which the humor consists not in intentional wit but in purely involuntary laughter arising from the character or the life of the people of that city. Absurdity is the essence of this type.[13] An example of it is found in Aelian's story of the paedagogue, the boy and the fig.[14] A paedagogue of Sybaris was escorting his young charge along the street when the boy found a fig and seized it for himself. The paedagogue beat the child roundly, snatched the fig from him and in the most laughable way ate it himself. Why Aelian was so amused by this story that he committed it to memory in order generously to *entertain* others by it seems a mystery.

Another type of story famous in antiquity was con-

---

[11] 1435–40.   [12] 1425–31.   [13] Rohde, *op cit.*, p. 588.
[14] Aelian, *Varia Historia*, XIV, 20.

nected with a city affiliated with Sybaris, namely, Miletus.
The Μιλησιακά were also associated with a definite person as
the Συβαριτικά were with Aesop, but Aristides seems to have
been both the narrator [15] of the tales of Miletus and the
historian, for he wrote in the second century B.C. a collection of these stories which were translated into Latin by
Cornelius Sisenna.[16] Their character was definite : they
were erotic stories of a lascivious type. Abbott well describes the Milesian tale. "In its commonest form it presented a single episode of every-day life. It brought out
some human weakness or foible. Very often it was a
story of illicit love. Its philosophy of life was : No man's
honesty and no woman's virtue are unassailable." [17]
Brevity and cynicism then are two essential features of
such a story. There is a familiar story of how horrified
the Parthian Surena was when the Milesian Tales were
found in the pack of an officer of Crassus in the Parthian
War of 53 B.C.[18]

Of course long before Aristides wrote his Μιλησιακά this
type of risqué story must have existed. Indeed Aristophanes again gives us evidence of the familiarity of such tales
in his time in the speech of Mnesilochus in the *Thesmo-
phoriazusae.*[19] Mnesilochus, a man disguised as a woman,
is telling a few "true stories" on the sex.

> For I myself, to mention no one else,
> Could tell a thousand plaguy tricks I've played
> On my poor husband ; I'll just mention one.
> We'd been but three days married ; I'm abed,
> Husband asleep beside me ; when my lover
> (I'd been familiar with him from a child)
> Came softly scratching at the outer door.
> I hear ; I know "the little clinking sound,"

---

[15] Lucian, *Amor.* 1.   [16] Ovid, *Trist.* II. 443-44.
[17] F. F. Abbott, *The Common People of Ancient Rome*, New York, 1911, p.
134.
[18] Plutarch, *Crass.* 32.   [19] *Thesm.* 476-90, 499-501.

And rise up stealthily, to creep downstairs.
Where go you, pray? says husband. *Where!* say I,
I've such a dreadful pain in my inside
I must go down this instant.   Go, says he.
He pounds his anise, juniper, and sage,
To still my pains : *I* seize the water-jug,
And wet the hinge, to still its creaking noise,
Then open, and go out : and I and lover
Meet by Aguieus and his laurel-shade,
Billing and cooing to our hearts' content.
Euripides has never found out that,
Nor how a wife contrived to smuggle out
Her frightened lover, holding up her shawl
To the sun's rays for husband to admire.

It is a far cry from Aristophanes to Apuleius, but in the later Latin authors the name *milesia* (*historia* or *fabula*) is applied to just such erotic *Novelle* as these or to stories of a merely amusing or frivolous type.   Apuleius in the beginning of his *Metamorphoses* declares he is going to string together various stories in the famous Milesian style.   So perhaps the romantic novel developed when a number of *milesiae* were all related as the experience of the hero, but there is not sufficient evidence to prove that Aristides' Μιλησιακά formed a connected novel.[20]   Not all the stories in Apuleius are erotic, but they aim as the author declares in his preface at giving entertainment, and they are narrated by the hero in an *ich-roman*.[21]

A special type of stories told with definite irony is concerned with the deception of husbands.   So many of them appear in Apuleius' novel that it is reasonable to infer that they are illustrations of the short, scandalous, erotic tales of Miletus.   They are in general not assigned to a special locality, but are laid "in a certain village."

[20] For summary of ancient evidence and modern theories see B. E. Perry, "An Interpretation of Apuleius' *Metamorphoses*," in *T.P.A.P.A.*, LVII (1926), pp. 253–58.
[21] L. C. Purser, *The Story of Cupid and Psyche as related by Apuleius*, London, 1910, Exc. 1 ; F. F. Abbott, *op. cit.*, 133–36 ; Apuleius, *Met.* I. 1.

Their origin is therefore uncertain, but their type is clear. They are often stories of humble life, the husband being a blacksmith, a baker, a fuller. The plot of several hinges on the unexpected return home of a husband and the ingenuity with which his guilty wife hides her faithlessness. The most striking stories might be assigned these titles : "The Lover under the Tub," "The Baker's Wife," "The Sandals under the Bed," "The Fuller's Wife," "The Murderess of Five."

But I am anticipating my conclusion by going too rapidly forward from the Μιλησιακά of Aristides to Apuleius' novel. Other local legends developed in Greek Asia besides those of Miletus and those of Sybaris in the west. From Cyprus came the stories of Myrrha (originally Phoenician) and of Arsinoe, from Lydia those of Niobe and of Nanis, daughter of King Croesus of Sardis, from Cyzicus the story of Clite, from the Hellespont the love-story of Hero and Leander. All these local stories and others Bruno Lavagnini has collected in his monograph *Le Origini del Romanzo greco.*

Lavagnini believes that a strong argument for his thesis that the Greek romances developed from local legends is given by their titles : Ἐφεσιακά and Βαβυλωνιακά of Xenophon of Ephesus and Xenophon of Antiochus, Αἰθιοπικά of Heliodorus, Κυπριακά of Xenophon of Cyprus, Ῥοδιακά, Κωακά, Θασιακά, romances of a Philippus of Amphipolis mentioned by Suidas.

Lavagnini thinks that the local legend developed into romance when the interest was transferred from the city to the individual, when in the narrative love and other human relations no longer were treated impersonally, largely for their genealogical interest, but for their human significance. The Greek romance because of its origin from local stories was always historical romance in the sense that the events were projected into a past, not definitely portrayed, but ideal and remote. Hence the Greek novel was not realistic.

The treatment of the story, however, was not idealistic, but under the influence of satire the novel was apt to deal with objective action rather than with inner drama. Man was regarded as the plaything of fortune and his struggles against it are depicted with no subtlety, but only in rhetorical speeches, put in the mouth of the suffering hero under the influence of the rhetorical schools.[22]

It is easy to see how out of the various local legends to which we have referred the few main types of stories developed which appear in classical literature. Probably first came animal stories and other folk-lore tales, then anecdotes of various cities, then travel stories of adventure and war, particularly after the time of Alexander ; next when in the Hellenistic Age the interest in the individual human being grew there appeared ironic stories of human relationships, often intensified by a macabre element, and pure love romances, usually tragic. These stories to be sure developed in no such exact chronological order as I have indicated, but in general folk-lore tales antedated ironic stories and love stories.

These types of course often overlap in one story. The narrator uses a local legend, gives it a human interest in relating it to one person, then seeing his hero as the toy of Fortune, he lets irony creep into his treatment and verges toward satire. Or, if his nature is romantic rather than satiric, he tells a serious love romance. Or he may vary his art of narration by using all types of stories and all moods of feeling in one novel and gain his unity by relating all the stories as experiences of one hero or of himself. So our two extant Latin novels developed. In

[22] B. Lavagnini, *Le Origini del Romanzo greco,* Pisa, 1921, pp. 98–104.

Petronius' *Satyricon* the life of a small town in Campania (Cumae) is pictured, often as seen through the eyes of a character from an unknown birthplace in Asia Minor, Trimalchio, an eastern-born *nouveau riche*. The narrative is told with the irony of the Sybaritic tale or of the Menippean satire from which the novel took its form. The type is that of the realistic novel. Apuleius' *Metamorphoses* is an *ich-roman* of an intellectual hero in search of a solution for the experiences of life through magic, sex and religion. It is a novel of adventure, based on a Greek prototype, and described by the author as written in the Milesian style, but actually it is a novel composed of many stories of different types and tone, united by the hero's personality and quest, and colored by romance and mysticism. An eastern religion finally frees the soul of the western adventurer.

To understand these two Latin novels more completely it is necessary to be familiar with their various precursors. Much has been written on the origins of the Greek romance, but little on the lineal ancestors of the two extant Latin novels. That is the reason for the particular study I am now undertaking of certain Oriental stories in earlier classical literature affiliated with types of stories in Petronius and Apuleius themselves. The material is found in the Greek and Latin historians, Herodotus, Xenophon and Livy, in Parthenius' little collection of *Love Romances* in Greek prose, in Plutarch's *Moralia,* in Phaedrus and Babrius, and hidden here and there in many other odd byways of ancient literature.

A study of animal stories and primitive myths would be too vast and too remote from our subject, but certain stories clearly arising from folk-lore should be mentioned. Two are illustrations of primitive wooing, another involves a primitive taboo.

Herodotus in his history of Scythia when he is describing a tribe called Sauromatae descended from Amazons and Scythians, gives a picture of racial wooing. After the Greeks defeated the Amazons at Thermodon, they sailed away in three ships with many captive Amazons. These women attacked the men at sea and threw them overboard. Then being unable to manage the ships they were driven ashore in the land of the Scythians. First of all they were fortunate in coming on a place where horses were reared and in seizing some for their invasion of the country.

The Scythians after a battle with them learned from the dead bodies that they were women instead of young men as they supposed and desired to have children by such valiant and stalwart females. So they sent a band of young men to encamp near them. These youths lived by hunting and plundering as the Amazons did. Finding that in the middle of the day the Amazons separated and scattered singly or in small groups, the young men did the same. At last one caught an Amazon who was alone, and raped her. She was by no means displeased, but indicated by signs that each should bring another person the next day. This was only the beginning of general unions. Finally they united their camps and each man took for wife his first mate.

The Amazons were the leaders in their new common life. They learned the men's language though the men could not learn theirs. They wisely refused to return to the Scythians' homes with them because they had no talent for women's crafts, but their skill was all in riding and hunting. And at last since they were afraid of the tribe because of their previous raids, they persuaded the men to migrate with them and make a new colony where they could develop their own life and customs. This they did. To preserve the character of their women, they had the rule that no girl should wed until she had slain an enemy. Some women being unable to fulfill this law died unwed.[23] Here is a story of origins, told with much detail and some conversation, depicting the union of two tribes, one supposed to be composed entirely of warrior women. It is a good illustration of myth emerging into *Novella*. If instead of having copulation and procreation as the themes, the story had recounted the individual wooing of one Scythian and one Amazon we should have a miniature romance.

In Livy's History of Rome, a prehistoric story of primitive wooing appears in the famous rape of the Sabine women.[24] It is an aetiological myth which grew up to explain the Sabine element in the early Latin state. The outline is that Romulus needing women to perpetuate the city he had founded and failing to secure them by negotiation from his haughty neighbors invited the tribes near to a great festival, the Consualia, and while the games were going on had their women seized and raped. Livy tells the story in a picturesque way, with a background of new Rome and the magnificence of the games, but the feeling involved of the women and their parents is only mob psychology. Romulus alone is individualized through his cunning plot, his speech of reconciliation to the women, his naming the tribes after them when they had proved instruments of peace between their husbands and fathers. Yet there is enough emotion in the narrative so that the possibilities of romantic or dramatic treatment are readily seen.[25]

Another story in Herodotus has clearly individualized

[23] Her. IV. 110–17.   [24] Livy, I. 9–10, 12–13.
[25] See "The Sabine Women," in *Plays* by Leonid Andréev, translated by C. L. Meader and F. N. Scott, New York, 1915.

characters, but the theme is as primitive as in these stories
of racial wooing : the taboo that a woman must not be
seen nude by anyone but her husband.   This is the famous tale of the wife of Candaules, ruler of Sardis and the
Lydians.[26]   Herodotus begins the story with a simple
statement of the motivation.   Now Candaules was madly
in love with his own wife and so believed her to be the
most beautiful of all women.   When he boasted of her
beauty to his favorite spearbearer, Gyges, he thought
Gyges looked incredulous, so he told Gyges that he would
give him proof of his words by letting him see her nude.
In spite of Gyges' horror and protests, the king insisted
and one night placed Gyges behind the door of his own
bed-chamber, telling him that after he had seen the queen
disrobe and she had turned toward the bed, he could slip
out unseen.

The queen, however, saw Gyges as he departed, but
that night she concealed her shame and said nothing, only
planned revenge.   The next day having summoned the
unsuspecting Gyges, she came to the point at once.

"Now Gyges I offer you a choice of two roads which
open before you.   Take which you wish.   Kill Candaules
and possess me and the kingdom of the Lydians, or at once
kill yourself that in future you may not obey Candaules'
orders and see what you ought not to see."

When the horrified Gyges found all his protests were
futile, he chose his own life.   The queen had her plan
ready.

"You shall attack Candaules from the very spot from
which he had you see me naked.   When he has gone to
sleep, you will do the deed."

So behind the same door of the royal chamber the same
body-guard was stationed, and when Candaules slept he

[26] Her. I. 8–12.

stole out and killed him.   Thus he got possession of queen and kingdom.

This is simple, rapid, dramatic narrative told in a very objective way for the sake of the plot.   The whole point of the vengeance is the insult to the queen in the breaking of the custom of the country that a man should see only his own wife.   There is no description of the woman's beauty, only of its effect on Candaules.   The taboo on seeing a woman naked is broken and nemesis follows. The dramatic element in the story comes from the horror of Gyges first at his monarch's daring to break with tradition, then at his queen's determination to maintain tradition even at the price of murder of her lord.[27]

Traces of a similar taboo appear in the story of Cupid and Psyche in Apuleius' novel.   The old fairy-story which was the kernel of Apuleius' beautiful, elaborated tale existed in many countries with the essential features the same, so we can not prove its eastern origin.   Certainly the *Märchen* existed in India.   The fundamental features of the story are a prince who has been transformed by evil powers into an animal, but at night resumes his own form and becomes the lover of a mortal girl who may be happy with him as long as she does not see his face. When she breaks this taboo, the lovers are separated and suffer countless hardships and labors before they are happily reunited.   In Apuleius there are hints that the lover had been transformed into a serpent but when Psyche breaks the taboo against seeing him, she discovers the God of Love.   Other traces of folk-lore in Apuleius are in the personification of inanimate objects like the talking tower and the gossiping sea-gull, and in the aid given to

[27] For a study of this story as romantic fiction, probably Greek in origin, with an element of the fable, see J. A. K. Thomson, *The Art of the Logos*, London, 1935, pp. 87-93.

the heroine by winds, insects and animals. A rich folk-lore foundation seems to root this flowering, tree-of-life story deep in the soil of mother earth.

In general the Oriental stories which appear in classical prose literature fall into two classes : ironic stories of human relations and romantic love-stories which are usually tragic. Certain stories are colored by both irony and sincere emotion and no grouping can be exact. Let us look first at some objective stories told chiefly for the sake of plot.

Such a one is that of Rhampsinitus, king of Egypt.[28]   It is a story of how the cleverness of a thief outwitted a king. Rhampsinitus was so wealthy that he had a special treasure-house built off his palace, opening only in the palace so that it should be safe. The builder however contrived a cunning scheme. He arranged a secret outside entrance by placing a stone so that it could easily be moved by one or two men. Before his death he bequeathed this secret to his two sons.

They at once put it to use and began to enrich themselves stealthily. But the king perceiving that his treasures were diminishing although the seals on the only door of the chamber were not broken, set traps about the vessels containing his wealth. At the next entrance of the thieves one was caught in the trap. He made his brother cut off his head and carry it away to save his own life and the secret.

The king on finding a headless robber caught, though the chamber door was unopened, had the corpse hung on the outer wall and stationed guards there to seize any who wept over it. The mother of the thief demanded that her living son should rescue the body. He with his usual ingenuity contrived to have a load of wine-skins break

[28] Her. II. 121.

down and burst before the guards, got them all drunk by the free use of the liquor, shaved their right cheeks by way of insult, and took his brother's body home to his mother.

The outwitted king then in anger decided to use his own daughter as a pawn, and made her act as a prostitute demanding as the price of her body that first each man should tell her the cleverest deed he had ever done and the greatest crime he had ever committed. The thief seeing how ingeniously this new trap was laid, determined to outwit the king. So he went to the princess in the dark of night with the arm of a man who had just died under his cloak. When she asked her questions, he confessed the cutting off his brother's head and the getting back the body by making the guards drunk. When the princess attempted to hold him till guards came, he slipped the dead man's arm into her hands and escaped.

On hearing this the king was so lost in admiration of the thief's cunning and courage that he made a proclamation promising him safety and reward if he would come to the king. The thief was bold enough to accept the offer and for his cleverness was given the princess as his wife.

This robber story is a rapid narrative of a lively plot, based on the theme of ingenuity and daring. It is full of macabre details : the headless thief, the hanging body and the severed arm. The irony appears in the comment on the brother taking the advice of the one in the trap, since he saw that it was good, and in the reversal of the king's emotion from anger at the thief to admiration of his ingenuity. The daring robber is a favorite type in stories of adventure and appears in several of the best stories in Apuleius.[29]

As famous and curious a story as the last is that of the

---

[29] For discussion of the story of Rhampsinitus as "a real Logos, a traditional Story, traditionally told," see J. A. K. Thomson, *op. cit.*, pp. 102-9.

woman of Ephesus, related by Petronius.[30]   Again the
plot is the main interest and the narrative is colored by
ironic presentation of the volatility of woman's emotion.
The setting is as bizarre as the other, where king's treasure-house, brothel and palace varied the scene.   Here an
underground tomb is the proscaenium of the comedy.
The heroine is a married woman of Ephesus so famous
for her virtue that women from other states traveled just
to look at her.   On the demise of her husband, the lady
accompanied by a faithful maid immured herself in his
tomb, to keep watch over his body.   She clearly planned
to starve herself to death so that she might follow him.
Neither relatives nor magistrates could dissuade her and
all began to mourn for her as a peerless example of virtue
and of devotion.   Five days passed, and each night the
maid lighted a lamp in the tomb and kept it burning.

Now the governor of the province had ordered that
some robbers should be crucified near the vault and a
guard set to watch the bodies.   This soldier, led by the
light, descended into the vault and found a most beautiful
woman mourning there.   Taking in the situation he
brought his supper into the tomb and tried first to comfort the Lady by the usual platitudes and then to persuade
her to eat.   The maid who soon succumbed to the temp-
tations of food and drink added her persuasions to the
soldier's and urged her Lady to begin life again.   Petronius remarks succinctly : "No one is reluctant to give ear
when urged to take food or keep alive," and adds : "You
know what naturally comes next."

The soldier having persuaded the Lady to live then
began to induce her to love, and the maid abetting him,
he was successful.   The tomb was the wedding-chamber.
The amorous soldier brought all the dainties he could to

[30] *Sat.* 111–13.

the tomb each night. While he was there with his Innamorata, the parents of one of the robbers came and stole
his body from the cross for burial. On discovering this
loss, the soldier declared he would kill himself rather than
wait for public disgrace and sentence ; and he bade his
Lady prepare another place in the vault for her lover.

The woman, "not less compassionate than pure," had
a ready answer : "May the gods forbid that I should behold at one time the corpses of both my husband and my
lover. I prefer that the dead should hang rather than
the living die." After this speech she ordered that her
husband's body be taken out of its coffin and hung on the
vacant cross. The soldier used the clever scheme of the
wise female and the next day the people wondered how
the dead man had ascended the cross.

A grewsome, soulless narrative of the gossamer texture
of woman's cloak of chastity ! It is told with a good deal
of atmosphere in the description of the dimly lighted
tomb and the bodies on the crosses. And the author lets
his personality intrude in ironic asides.

These are enough illustrations of *Novelle* told for interest of episode, plot, or behavior, uncolored by emotion,
sometimes enlivened by ironic comment of narrator.
The other common type of short story which appears in
ancient prose fiction is the romantic. Its theme is the
love of a man and a woman. Its end is usually tragic.
These small romances are embedded in Herodotus and
Xenophon, constitute a whole book of Parthenius' writings, are scattered throughout Apuleius' novel and are
found in Phaedrus, Plutarch and other writers of different
ages. Jealousy and treachery are often motivating forces
in them. Occasionally there is a tale of pure romantic
love.

Herodotus, when he has finished his magnificent history

of the Persian wars and rounded out his drama to the final expulsion of the eastern invaders from Greece, suddenly shifts his scene to the Persian court at Sardis and gives a picture of the intrigues, cruelties and corruptions of court life there.[31]   He labels the story himself :

"Such was the story of the love of Xerxes and the death of Masistes."   Godley believes this "an example of Herodotus' supreme art," for the chapters portray the horrors of Persian absolutism, the fear of the caprice and cruelty of Oriental despots that nerved the Greeks to resist their dominion.[32]

The scene is Sardis, where Xerxes had been ever since his defeat at Salamis.   The time is shortly after the arrival of the survivors of the battle of Mycale, among them Masistes, the brother of King Xerxes.   The king had fallen in love with his brother's wife, but all his wooing had failed to win her and he would not use force to possess her because she was the wife of his brother.   So he made a plan by which he hoped indirectly to secure her : he married his own son, Darius, to the daughter of this lady and Masistes and invited them to his palace at Susa.   There he became enamored of the young bride, Artaÿnte, forgot her mother and won the daughter.

His intrigue was revealed through the vanity of the girl. Xerxes' wife, Amestris, had woven a large, many colored cloak for him, and Xerxes, delighted with the gift, went to Artaÿnte, wearing it.   Now Xerxes made the mistake of asking the young woman what she wished in return for her favors.   The girl because a fatality was pursuing her and her family made him promise to give her whatever she requested.   Then she asked for his new cloak. Xerxes fearing his wife offered her instead cities, gold in

[31] Her. IX. 108–13.
[32] A. D. Godley, *Herodotus,* in *The Loeb Classical Library,* IV, p. XVII.

abundance, an army to command herself, but Artaÿnte insisted on his keeping his oath, and so received the cloak.

When the queen heard she had the robe, she became madly enraged at the girl's mother, believing her the guilty one, and plotted her destruction. At the royal banquet on the king's birthday when the monarch must grant every request made to him, Amestris demanded of the king that his brother's wife be given to her. Xerxes, perceiving his wife's suspicion and purpose, was most reluctant, but being bound by the custom of the country gave her up and told Amestris to do what she wished.

Then he sent for Masistes and ordered him to give up his own wife and marry Xerxes' daughter. Masistes, horrified, refused. The dialogue between the brothers is brief and violent.

Xerxes concluded his proposal thus : "Take my daughter to your home and bed. And put aside the wife whom you now have, for it is not my will that you should live with her."

Masistes in amazement replied :

"My lord, what terrible word do you utter, giving me orders about my wife ! She is the mother of my young sons and daughters, one of whom you married to your own son. And I love her. Do you command me to put her away and marry your daughter ? O king, I recognize the great honor you confer, but I will do neither of these things. Do not force me to carry out your wish. You will find another son-in-law not less worthy. Permit me to live with my own wife."

Xerxes in rage retorted :

"Very well : this is what has happened to you, Masistes. I would not give you my daughter now, and you shall not live any longer with your wife, that you may learn to receive orders."

Masistes then departed with a last word : "Monarch, you have not yet destroyed me."

But during the conversation, Amestris had had Xerxes' guards torture the wife of Masistes. She cut off her breasts and threw them to the dogs. She cut off her nose, her ears, her lips. She cut out her tongue. Then she sent home the mutilated woman. That was the wife Masistes found when he reached his house. Masistes gathered together all his sons and their friends and started forth toward Bactra, where he was hyparch, planning a revolution against the king. But Xerxes sent an army after him which overtook him and slew Masistes, his sons and their companions. "This is the story of the love of Xerxes and the death of Masistes."

If this story is war propaganda, at least it is told in a convincing way. And out of its lusts, its frivolities and its barbarities emerges the touching and tragic story of Masistes, his wife and his family : first the corruption of his young daughter who was married to Darius, then her innocent and unwitting destruction of her whole family through her frivolous demand for Xerxes' bright robe. The irony of Greek tragedy plays around the words of Masistes to Xerxes, "Monarch, you have not destroyed me yet," when it is seen that his wife in that hour is being tortured and it proves that there is no redress or escape for him from his brother's power.

One of the most perfect romances found in classical writings is the story of Abradatas of Susa and Panthea, told in Xenophon's *Education of Cyrus*.[33] It is "the first love-story in European prose." [34] Rohde thinks that it was a pure invention of Xenophon as later versions de-

[33] Xen. *Cyr.* IV. 6, 11 ; V. 1, 2–18 ; VI. 1, 31–50 ; VI. 3, 35–36 ; VI. 4, 1–11 ; VII. 3, 2–16.
[34] L. Whibley, *A Companion to Greek Studies*, Cambridge, 1916, p. 155.

pend on his narrative.[35]   The story is so seldom read that
I am going to recount it here.   It is told, almost as a
modern serial story, at intervals through the narrative of
Cyrus' wars with Assyria and Lydia.   But cut out from
its background of war and history it is a complete and
rather long love-story.

After the war with the Assyrians, the Medes in dividing
the spoils, selected for Cyrus the finest tent, two talented
music girls and a lady reputed to be the most beautiful
woman in Asia.   This was Panthea, wife of Abradatas
prince of Susa.   When the Assyrian camp was taken, her
husband happened to be away on a diplomatic mission to
the king of Bactria.   Cyrus assigned the care of Panthea
to his lifelong friend, Araspas, a Mede, until he himself
should take her.   Araspas on finding that Cyrus had not
seen the lady, described his first impression of her :

"I saw her when we chose her for you, Cyrus.   When
we entered her tent, we could not identify her at first, for
she sat on the ground among her maids, clothed even as
they.   But soon we knew her even in that garb and bowed
to earth.   And when we bade all stand, she was distinguished by her height, her nobility, and her bearing.   We
saw that her tears were falling on her robe.   The oldest of
our band spoke : 'Take heart, Lady.   We hear that your
husband is noble and valiant.   But know that we are
selecting you for a hero no less handsome, wise and powerful.   For to our minds Cyrus surpasses all men and you
are to be his.'

"Now when the lady heard these words, she uttered a
loud cry and while all her maids shrieked with her, she
rent her robe from top to bottom.   So we saw her face,
her side, her arms.   Believe me, Cyrus, we all thought

[35] Rohde, *op. cit.*, p. 139 note 1. Cf. Lucian, *Imag.* 10 ; Philostratus, *Imag.*
II. 9.

her the most beautiful mortal woman in Asia.   You must see her for yourself."

To Araspas' surprise, Cyrus refused, saying that such beauty would call him back again and again, and gazing at the Lady he would forget his duties.   With this beginning, Cyrus and Araspas engaged in a long philosophical discussion about the effects of beauty and love. Araspas maintained that love is a matter of free will ; and beauty cannot compel a man to act against his reason. Cyrus replied that love may be like slavery or like a disease, and for those who surrender to it there is no escape. Araspas protested, affirming that only the weak could be so dominated, for the noble and the good control their desires.   Cyrus finally commended his friend's principles and entrusted Panthea to him but with a word of warning against the fire which beauty seen too oft might kindle.

"Trust me, Cyrus," said Araspas.   "For if I always keep gazing at the Lady, I will never be so overcome as to do anything that I ought not to do."

What Cyrus had anticipated happened.   Panthea's beauty and nobility, her thoughtfulness for her guard especially when he fell ill, his sense of pleasing her all helped to make Araspas fall in love.   As time went on he could no longer keep silent so he made known his state to Panthea and begged her to give him herself.   She repelled him in horror, for she was faithful to her absent husband and indeed loved him ardently.   She did not accuse Araspas to Cyrus at once, for she did not wish to estrange friends.   But when Araspas threatened her with violence, then in terror she sent her eunuch to Cyrus to tell him her plight.

Cyrus laughed heartily at this tale of the hero who claimed to be stronger than love and sent Artabazus back with the eunuch to warn Araspas against doing violence to such a lady. He sent also the message that if Araspas could win Panthea's heart she should be his. Artabazus added a moral lecture of his own about the betrayal of a trust which reduced Araspas to tears and terror. On hearing of this, Cyrus sent for his friend and with true magnanimity assured him of his confidence and of his friendship. The king then proposed that under cover of their rumored estrangement over the Lady, Araspas should pretend to flee from him and go over to the enemy's country as a spy.

"An excellent plan," said Araspas. "I know even my friends would think that I was running away from you in fear of punishment. I will set out at once."

"And will you be able to leave beautiful Panthea?" asked Cyrus.

"Yes, Cyrus," replied his friend, "for Love has taught me that I have two souls, one good, one bad, and each tries to gain the mastery. Now my good genius has taken you as her ally and is ruling my life."

This is the end of the love-story of Araspas. Even Panthea believed that Araspas had deserted Cyrus for the enemy. So she proposed to Cyrus to send for her husband, Abradatas, and she assured him that Abradatas would be a more faithful friend than Araspas. She declared that she knew her husband would be glad to join his arms, for the present king of his own country had once tried to separate her husband and herself. Cyrus accepted her proposal.

When Abradatas received his wife's letter, he was overjoyed and proceeded at once with a thousand horsemen to Cyrus. Cyrus on learning from the sentries that Abradatas had arrived, ordered them to escort him at once to his wife. And when Abradatas and his Panthea met, they clung to each other in a long embrace, for they had not hoped to see each other again. Then Panthea told of Cyrus' courtesy, his self-control, his compassion for her.

When Abradatas heard her story, he asked : "What can I ever do, Panthea, to show Cyrus my gratitude for you and for myself ?"

Panthea answered : "What else but try to be such a friend to him as he has been to you !"

The loyal devotion which Abradatas then offered Cyrus was accepted and Abradatas began to equip a fine cavalry contingent for the war with Lydia. Araspas came back and made report to Cyrus on the condition of the enemy. (No word was said about his love.) And finally all preparations were made for the battle. Abradatas had attained by lot the dangerous post which he coveted, the command against the Egyptians. Now the moment of his farewell to Panthea came, for his chariot with its eight horses stood ready in splendid array. As he started to put on his old armor Panthea surprised him with a new equipment, corselet, helmet, arm-pieces, bracelets all of gold, a long purple tunic and a hyacinth-colored plume for his helmet.

"My wife," exclaimed Abradatas, "you have sacrificed your jewels for my armor."

"Not my most precious jewel, I swear," answered Panthea. "For you are my greatest glory."

Then she helped him put on the armor, and there were tears on her cheeks which she could not hide. Very handsome and free Abradatas looked as he started to mount his chariot, but now Panthea signalled to all to withdraw, while she said good-bye :

"Abradatas, if any woman ever loved her husband more than her own soul, I am that wife. I need not say more. My past life is better proof to you of my love than any words. Yet out of my love I swear to you now that I would rather die with you, a hero, than live with you, a coward. For I deem us both worthy of the noblest fate. And we both owe much to Cyrus, who when I was a captive and his prize of war, did not dishonor me but guarded me for you as if I were his brother's wife."

Abradatas much moved put his hand upon her head and looking up to heaven prayed :

"Grant, O great Zeus, that I may prove myself a husband worthy of Panthea and a friend worthy of Cyrus who has honored us both."

Then he mounted his chariot. Panthea pressed her lips on the car. As Abradatas drove away, he called back : "Be brave, Panthea. Go back now. Good-bye."

After the battle was over and the victory won, Cyrus, as he was distributing the spoils, called to some of his officers : "Tell me, has any one seen Abradatas ? I marvel that he does not appear."

"O king," answered one of the aides, "Abradatas is no longer alive. He died as he charged in his chariot against the Egyptians. And even now his wife is driving with her dead to a hill near the river Pactolus. There Abradatas' eunuchs and servants are digging his grave."

In a moment Cyrus had given orders and was off with a thousand horses and many offerings for the dead hero. He found Panthea sitting on the ground beside her husband's body. Cyrus wept and crying : "O brave and faithful soul, hast thou gone and left us ?" he clasped the hand of his friend. But the hand came away in his grasp, for it had been cut off by an Egyptian sword. Horror overcame Cyrus. But Panthea taking the hand from Cyrus kissed it and fitted it on again and said :

"All his body is in that state, Cyrus. But why should you see it ?" . . . I am the cause of his suffering and perhaps you too, for I urged him to be a worthy friend to you and he wished only to please you.   Now he has died an honorable death and I who encouraged him sit here alive."

For some time Cyrus wept silently.   Then he found voice to say : "This man, Lady, has the most beautiful of fates.   He died victorious.   He shall have such a monument as befits a brave hero.   And you shall not be left desolate.   For on account of your nobility I will honor you and give you an escort to conduct you wherever you wish.   Only make known to me to whom you wish to be sent."

Panthea answered : "Be assured, Cyrus, that I will not conceal from you the name of the one to whom I wish to go."

Cyrus then departed, grieving over the fate of his friend. Panthea ordered the eunuchs to withdraw that she might mourn her husband as she wished.   She had her nurse wait and directed her when she was dead, to cover her husband and herself with one mantle.   The nurse tried to dissuade her from her purpose but when she saw Panthea was angered, she sat down weeping.   Panthea then drew forth a dagger which she had long ago secured and laying her head on her husband's breast she killed herself. The nurse with a loud wail covered them both as Panthea had ordered.

When Cyrus heard of the deed, he hastened back to see if he could be of aid.   The three eunuchs, perceiving what had happened, drew their daggers and stabbed themselves on the spot where their mistress had ordered them to stand.   Cyrus made lament over Panthea and in course of time, that both she and her husband might receive fitting honors, he had a great monument erected over their burial place.

The tale told is pure romance.   It is a love-story set against a background of war.   All the characters are

noble.   Heroine and hero have glamorous beauty.   The
great warrior who might have dishonored the captive
heroine proves a generous friend.   The guard who falls
in love with her gains self-control through the example
of his king and his own philosophical musings.   The
friendship of Cyrus and Abradatas is a virile counterpart
to the love between wife and husband.   And the touching
little speeches of Panthea as she says farewell to her hero
or kisses his severed hand gain poignancy from their sin-
cerity.   The tragic ending of the story is eased by the fact
that even in death the lovers were not divided.

Livy, the first great historian of Rome, uses *Novelle* in
his historical narrative almost as freely as Herodotus had
done.   Some of them, Horatius at the bridge, Scaevola
putting his hand in the fire, the death of Virginia, the rape
of Lucretia, have become so familiar in various literary
treatments that it is almost forgotten that Livy is their
source.   Yet the art with which he told these little stories
is what established their dramatic character and their
poignancy.[36]   The story of the traitor girl was never presented with more horror than when Horatius stabbed his
sister, declaring that not even tears for a dead lover were
permitted when that lover was an enemy.[37]   No crime-
stained queen ever seemed more barbaric than Tullia be-
spattered with the blood of her murdered father as she
had her chariot driven over his body.[38]   And memorable
are those dead bodies of Lucretia and Virginia displayed
in the forum, one a noble woman who after being raped
killed herself to clear her honor ; the other a plebeian girl,
stabbed by her father to save her from a like fate.   The
very simplicity of Livy's narrative brings tears for such
things.[39]

[36] See H. Taine, *Essai sur Tite Live*, Paris, 1904, pp. 274–78.
[37] Livy, I. 26.   [38] Livy, I. 46–48.   [39] Livy, I. 57–59; III. 44–48.

Perhaps the Roman historian was influenced in the use of *Novelle* for the development of his art of narration by the example of Herodotus.[40] Livy's stories are certainly pertinent for his Roman history and the eastern coloring of certain ones is involved in the historical connections of Rome with the East. If the Etruscans came from Lydia as the ancients generally believed, then the stories of the crimes of Tullia and of the lust of Sextus Tarquinius may have an Oriental tinge. Certainly one of the maddest of Livy's romantic stories is eastern to the core. That is the story of Sophonisba.[41] Probably no story in Livy has been used more often in later literature.[42]

The time was the second Punic War, 203 B.C. Scipio had brought the war into Africa. Two rival African kings figured in the struggle : Syphax who had married a daughter of Hasdrubal, Sophonisba, and had joined the side of the Carthaginians ; and Masinissa who, driven out of his kingdom by Syphax had joined the Romans. Scipio, Laelius and Masinissa defeated the Carthaginians in several battles and finally Laelius and Masinissa took Syphax captive. Masinissa, with Oriental cunning, asked Laelius if he might not be allowed to go ahead to Cirta, the capital of Numidia, his former kingdom, with the cavalry and their captive, Syphax, since he felt sure he could take the citadel. Laelius consented.

Those of us who have visited Cirta, the modern Constantine, know the impregnable site of that high rock-acropolis, guarded by the deep gorge of the Rummel. Masinissa's strategy was necessary to take it. He called the leading men of the city outside to a conference before he gave them the real news. When pressure and per-

---

[40] See J. A. K. Thomson, *op. cit.*, p. 87.   [41] Livy, XXX. 12–15.
[42] See A. Andrae, "Sophonisbe in der französichen Tragödie mit Berücksichtigung der Sophonisbebearbeitungen in anderen Litteraturen," in *Zeitschrift für neufranzösische Sprache und Litteratur*, 2–10, Supp. 6, 1891.

suasion failed to induce them to surrender, he suddenly displayed King Syphax in chains. Horror and terror then opened the city gates as the guards fled.

Masinissa protecting all exits rode at full speed to take the palace. At the very threshold as he entered the vestibule, Sophonisba met him. At once perceiving the situation and knowing from Masinissa's gait and armor that he must be the king, she fell at his feet and burst forth into an eloquent appeal that he should make his own decision about her fate as a captive and save her from ever being given over alive to the Romans. She said that she as a Numidian could trust him, a fellow-countryman, and as the daughter of Hasdrubal she must dread a Roman conqueror. She was very beautiful and young. The Numidians are mad lovers. The conqueror fell in love with Sophonisba at first sight. He promised that she should never fall into the hands of the Romans and he married her that day before Laelius and Scipio arrived.

Laelius, reaching Cirta just after the union, was greatly enraged and wished to tear Sophonisba from her wedding bed to send her to Scipio. Masinissa finally persuaded him to leave to Scipio the decision as to whose wife Sophonisba was. When all arrived at Scipio's camp, that general had a delicate piece of diplomacy before him with the two Numidian kings.

First he let the captive Syphax have audience with him and speak freely. The prisoner confessed that in madness he had broken his alliance with the Roman people, but he declared that the cause of his insane actions was the Carthaginian woman whom he had married ; that fury and pest had left him no peace until she had inflamed him against his Roman friends, and his only comfort in his present misfortunes was that the accursed woman had gone over to his worst enemy to be his torment.

Although Scipio saw that Syphax was making this denunciation more from the sting of passion than from
hatred of an enemy, he yet was horrified that the marriage
of Sophonisba to Masinissa had taken place the day her
former husband was captured and in his own palace. So
next he had a private interview with Masinissa and after
praising highly his military success, he talked to him
quietly on the theme that he who ruleth his spirit wins a
far greater glory than he who conquers Cirta. He declared that he himself had aimed to make his own greatest
virtues self-control and mastery of passion. Now Syphax
had been conquered under the auspices of the Roman people ; hence he himself, his wife, his kingdom, his territory,
towns and inhabitants were the booty of the Romans ;
and the king and his wife should be sent to Rome to await
the will of senate and people. Masinissa must control his
spirit and not wipe out his glorious record by a great mistake.

Masinissa flushed and wept. Then he declared that he
would hold himself under his general's orders, but he
begged him that he might keep his given word. After
this he departed to his own tent. There those outside
heard him groaning and sobbing for some time. Finally
sending for a faithful slave he ordered him to prepare a
cup of poison and carry it to Sophonisba with the message :
"Masinissa would gladly have kept his first vows to his
wife. But since those in power prevent, he keeps his
second vow that she shall not go alive into the power of
the Romans. Let her remember her father, the ruler,
her native land, the two kings to whom she has been wed,
and make her own decision."

When the messenger with the poison had come to
Sophonisba she said : "I accept the wedding present and

it pleases me since my husband could give his wife no greater gift. Yet carry back this word : that I would have died better if I had not been married at the hour of my funeral."

She spoke calmly and with no sign of distress she drained the goblet.

Scipio on hearing the news, fearing for the violent nature of Masinissa, summoned him, told him his regret that he had heaped one horror on another, but upbraided him gently. The next day he held an assembly and did Masinissa public honor, addressing him as king, loading him with encomia, and presenting him with golden crown and patera, curule chair and ivory sceptre, embroidered toga and tunic ; and he declared that no Roman conqueror ever received higher honors on his triumph than this one ally of Rome was receiving that day. By this public honor Masinissa was diverted from his private grief to political ambition.

Now this is history, but it is also romance. It is a Numidian love-story told with a hint of the fire of the East and of the emotional complications when East meets West. The contrast between the cold, self-restrained Scipio and the passionate, young Masinissa is well played off and Sophonisba's own hot-headed Punic nationalism makes her an effective *casus belli*. Livy's story is both effective in itself and valuable in its historical truth of the difficulties of alliances between Occident and Orient. No Latin story was used more often in the Renaissance.

Most significant for the study of classical prose *Novelle* is the collection of *Love Romances* written by Parthenius of Nicaea in Bithynia. Parthenius wrote in Greek chiefly elegiac poems. He was taken captive by Cinna when the Romans defeated Mithridates and his life was spared be-

cause of his value as a teacher, indeed he was said to have
been Vergil's tutor in Greek. He was an intimate friend
of the poet Cornelius Gallus and dedicated to him his
Love Romances that he might use their material for epic
or elegiac verses. The stories therefore purport to be
bare skeletons for Gallus to cover with flesh, blood and
garments. But some already are colored by feeling that
no rattling bones could evoke.

The origins of the stories are stated. The sources are
both prose and poetry : epic, elegiac verse and drama,
historical and philosophical prose. Mythology is drawn
on, but well-known stories are not used. Certain stories
are connected with historical characters. Some are
clearly local legends.

The general characteristics of the *Love Romances* are
well summarized by M. M. Crump in her book on *The
Epyllion*.[43]

"Twenty-five end with the death — usually violent — of
one or both of the principal characters. The remaining
eleven, though not actually ending in tragedy, are characterized by unfaithfulness on the part of the hero or
heroine, or by some incident of violence or treachery.
Three only can be said to have happy endings. Certain
incidents recur several times ; in six cases a girl is forsaken
by her lover ; murder and accidental death appear fre-
quently, and there are six instances of murder of kinsmen ; suicide occurs eight times. In six of the tales the
plot turns on unnatural affection, and the same motive
occurs incidentally in three more. In five the chief
motive is the love of a girl for an enemy, and three of these
end with the heroine's betrayal of her father to her lover.

[43] M. M. Crump, *The Epyllion from Theocritus to Ovid*, Oxford, 1931,
p. 108.

It will be seen that violence, treachery and unfaithfulness are constantly recurring themes."

As typical may be described the six connected with the city of Miletus, for they seem to link with Aristides' Μιλησιακοὶ λόγοι and with the type of tragic love-romances which we have been reviewing.

One is a story of the oracle of Didyma near Miletus.[44] Lyrcus of Caunus went to consult the oracle because he and his wife had no children. The oracle prophesied that he would have a child by the first woman with whom he lay after leaving the shrine. Overjoyed he started home, but on the way he was entertained over night at Bybastus. That night his host, who had heard of the oracle, when his guest was drunk, united with him his own daughter, for he wished grandsons and the girl had fallen in love with the stranger. Lyrcus in the morning was very angry at this treachery, but finally on departing gave his belt to the girl to use as an identification token if she ever had a son who wished to see his father. This happened in due time, but before that the story got out at Caunus and Lyrcus' father-in-law made war on Lyrcus and his followers. Lyrcus' wife, Hilebra, however, stood by Lyrcus.

Another story of the town of Caunus is of the founder who named the town for himself.[45] Byblis and Caunus were sister and brother who lived in Miletus. Byblis fell madly in love with her brother and when he rejected her and left home, she hanged herself from an oak-tree. Another version of the tragic love of brother and sister is told with more elaboration of Leucippus of Lycia.[46]

[44] The Love Romances of Parthenius, with an English translation by S. Gaselee in The Loeb Classical Library, New York, 1924, I.
[45] Ibid., XI.   [46] Ibid., V.

A typical story of treachery is that of Polycrite of Naxos and her lover.[47]   Her city was being besieged by the men of Miletus.   The girl, Polycrite, had been left in a temple outside the city.   There she captivated Diognetus, leader of the Erythraeans on the side of Miletus.   When he kept wooing her, she promised her love if he would swear to do whatever she asked.   She asked him to relieve the blockade of her city and end its wars.   After a night's reflection Diognetus agreed and sent a message on a lead tablet in a loaf of bread to Polycrite's brother who was in command of Naxos promising to aid him if he made a sally forth that night.   This plot was successful but in the battle Diognetus was killed.   The next day the Naxians wishing to honor Polycrite presented her with so many head-dresses and girdles that the weight of them as they pressed upon her suffocated her.   She was given a public funeral and Diognetus' body was burned with hers on one funeral pyre.

Usually in these stories of treachery the girl is the traitor to her country.   Leucophrye fell in love with Leucippus who was besieging her father's city, and for her love betrayed her own city.[48]   The same story is told of Pisidice and Achilles,[49] and of Nanis, daughter of Croesus, and Cyrus.[50]

There are three stories of faithless wives of Miletus. Neaera, wife of Hypsicreon, fell in love with her husband's dear friend, Promedon of Naxos, who was their guest.   At first he refused her advances.   When her husband was away, she went to Promedon's room, had her maids lock them in.   Finally he yielded.   The next day in shame he fled to Naxos.   Neaera followed him.   This caused a war between Miletus and Naxos.[51]

47 *Ibid.*, IX.   48 *Ibid.*, V.   49 *Ibid.*, XXI.
50 *Ibid.*, XXII.   51 *Ibid.*, XVIII.

Another Milesian tale of the same sort is that of Cleoboea, wife of Phobius, ruler of Miletus.[52] She fell in love with a young prince, Antheus, who had been sent as a hostage from Halicarnassus to her husband. When Antheus out of reverence for Zeus, god of hospitality, and respect for her husband, his host, refused her love, she drove a pet partridge down a deep well, asked Antheus to go down to get it for her, then pushed a huge stone down upon him which killed him. Finally, in horror at her crime and mad with passion she hanged herself.

The best of these traitor women stories, indeed perhaps the finest of all that Parthenius recorded is the story of Herippe of Miletus, her husband, Xanthus, and the Gaul who carried her off. I quote S. Gaselee's translation.[53]

"During the invasion of Ionia by the Gauls and the devastation by them of the Ionian cities, it happened that on one occasion at Miletus, the feast of the Thesmophoria was taking place, and the women of the city were congregated in the temple a little way outside the town. At that time a part of the barbarian army had become separated from the main body and had entered the territory of Miletus ; and there, by a sudden raid, it carried off the women.

"Some of them were ransomed for large sums of silver and gold, but there were others to whom the barbarians became closely attached, and these were carried away : among these latter was one Herippe, the wife of Xanthus, a man of high repute and of noble birth among the men of Miletus, and she left behind her a child two years old.

"Xanthus felt her loss so deeply that he turned a part of his best possessions into money and, furnished with two thousand pieces of gold, first crossed to Italy : he was there furthered by private friends and went on to Marseilles, and thence into the country of the Celts ; and finally, reaching the house where Herippe lived as the wife of one of the chief men of that nation, he asked to be taken in. The Celts received him with the utmost hospitality : on entering the house he saw his wife, and she, flinging her arms about his neck, welcomed him with all the marks of affection.   Immediately the Celt appeared, Herippe related to him her husband's journeyings, and how he had come to pay a ransom for her.   He was delighted at the devotion of Xanthus, and, calling together his nearest relations to a banquet, entertained him warmly ; and when they had drunk deep, placed his wife by his side, and asked him through an interpreter how great was his whole fortune.   'It amounts to a thousand pieces of gold,' said Xanthus ; and the barbarian then bade him divide it into four parts — one each for himself, his wife, and his child, and the fourth to be left for the woman's ransom.

"After he had retired to his chamber, Herippe upbraided Xanthus vehemently for promising the barbarian this great sum of money which he did not possess, and told him that he would be in a position of extreme jeopardy if he did not fulfil his promise : to which Xanthus replied that he even had another thousand gold pieces which had been hidden in the soles of his servants' boots, seeing that he could scarcely have hoped to find so reasonable a barbarian, and would have been likely to need an enormous ransom for her.   The next day she went to the Celt and informed him of the amount of money which Xanthus had in his possession, advising him to put him to death : she added that she preferred him, the Celt, far above both her native country and her child, and, as for Xanthus, that she utterly abhorred him.   Her tale was far from pleasing to the Celt, and he decided to punish her : and so, when Xanthus was anxious to be going, he most amiably accompanied him for the first part of his journey, taking Herippe with them ; and when they arrived at the limit of the Celts' territory, he announced that he wished to perform a sacrifice before they separated from one another.   The victim was brought up, and he bade Herippe hold it : she did so, as she had been accustomed to do on previous occasions, and he then drew his sword, struck with it, and cut off her head.   He then explained her treachery to Xanthus, telling him not to take in bad part what he had done, and gave him all the money to take away with him."

These typical *Novelle* from Parthenius show the character of his *Love Romances*.   Their theme was love, usually unhappy love.   "A conflict between duty and passion occurs in many of the tales," as Miss Crump notes.[54] The main interest is in the psychology of the characters.

[54] Crump, *op. cit.*, p. 113.

The fact that the stories were recommended to Gallus for poetic treatment, particularly in elegiac verse, shows that the stories were regarded by Parthenius as fundamentally colored by emotion.

In Plutarch's *Moralia,* the section on *Mulierum Virtutes, The Bravery of Women,* contains many miniature stories of collective heroism or individual brave deeds. Plutarch says in his preface that the stories are gathered for his friend Clea, a priestess at Delphi, to continue a conversation which they had on the equality of the sexes. He has then a thesis to prove by illustration : that the virtues of men and women are the same. And he has a standard to flaunt, with the device : "Faith in the love of beauty in man's soul." Plutarch's women therefore are for the most part faithful and gallant heroines who display intelligence, loyalty and courage for their husbands and their countries. A few illustrations will show his themes and simple, narrative style.

There was a war between the Ionians of Miletus and Myus, but it was not without truce and communication. Indeed the women of Myus went to certain religious festivals at Miletus. A noble Milesian youth, Phrygius, there fell in love with a maiden from Myus called Pieria. And he was racking his brains to think what he could do to find favor in her sight. The girl gave him a hint, saying : "If only you would make it possible for me to come here often with many companions !" Phrygius quickly understanding that she wished friendship and peace for their cities, stopped the war. For this Pieria gained such great honor in both cities that still the women of Miletus pray that their husbands may love them as Phrygius did Pieria.[55]

In the story of the Women of Melos there is to be sure

[55] Plutarch, *Mul. Virt.* xvi.

a traitor girl who betrayed her country, but this is ex-
tenuated by the fact that she betrayed a Carian city to
Greeks and the main point of the story is the courage of
Greek women at a fateful banquet.   A colony of Melians
had been led by Nymphaeus to Caria, near the city
of Cryassus.   The Carians at first were friendly but as
time went on they became jealous of the prosperity of
the Greeks and planned to destroy all the men at a
banquet.

Now a Carian girl, Caphene, who had fallen in love
with Nymphaeus, revealed the plot to him.   So he told
the Carians that the Greeks did not go to dinner parties
without their women.   When the women too were invited, Nymphaeus directed each to conceal a sword in
her bosom and to sit beside the man of her family, who
must go unarmed.   When the Greeks saw the Carians
give the signal for destruction, each Greek man seized a
sword from the woman beside him and thus armed
fought and conquered the Carians.   Thus the Greeks
got possession of the land.   Caphene was married to
Nymphaeus and greatly honored.   And all must admire
the courage of the Greek women who played their parts
so bravely.[56]

The other two illustrations which I have selected from
Plutarch are tales of faithful wives.   Both end in murder.
In each the straight narrative is enlivened by a short
speech at the end.

The story of Chiomara is a story of the war in Asia in
189 B.C., when the Romans defeated the Galatians.   Chiomara, wife of Ortiagon, was taken captive and the Roman officer who got possession of her ravished her as is
the custom of soldiers in wartime.   He was an ignorant
fellow with no self-control when lust or money was

[56] *Ibid.,* VII.

involved. He was destroyed by love of money. He agreed to accept a large ransom in gold for the woman. The negotiations were carried on at a certain river. The officer had just received the ransom and was bidding Chiomara an affectionate farewell, when a Galatian at a signal from the lady struck off the head of the Roman. Chiomara picked up the head, wrapped it in her robe, carried it to her husband and threw it down before him. When he in amazement exclaimed : "My wife, loyalty is beautiful," she replied : "Yes, but it is more beautiful to have only one man alive who has been my bed-fellow." The cool ferocity and austere virtue of the Galatian women are crystallized in that single sentence.[57]

The story of Camma is the most famous of these tales by Plutarch. It was dramatized by Tennyson in a play called "The Cup" which had a run of over one hundred and thirty nights when it was presented in the Lyceum Theater by Henry Irving. Even here in its simplest form it has a dramatic quality.

In Galatia there were two very powerful rulers, Sinatus and Sinorix, who were distantly related. Sinatus had a wife who was famous for her beauty and her character. She was self-controlled, devoted to her husband, intelligent, and beloved by her inferiors for her kindness to them. As she was a priestess of Artemis she was often seen publicly in magnificent robes in processions and at sacrifices.

So Sinorix fell in love with her and being unable to win her by persuasion or force while her husband lived, he did a terrible deed : he treacherously killed Sinatus. Not long after he pressed his suit for Camma's hand. She was serving in the temple. He frankly stated that he was a better man than her first husband and had made way

[57] *Ibid.,* XXII.

with him simply because of his own passion for her. Camma made no violent refusal and seemed to soften as time went on, especially as relatives and friends urged her to accept Sinorix, for he was very powerful.

Finally she consented and summoned him to the temple that they might make their vows in the presence of the goddess. When he came, she received him in friendly fashion. Then she led him to the altar, poured a libation from a bowl, drank herself from the bowl and bade Sinorix drink the rest. It was a poisoned cup. When she saw that he had drunk, she gave a glad cry and kneeling before the goddess, said: "I call thee to witness, goddess most adored, that for this day I have lived since the murder of Sinatus, and I have had no joy in life but the hope of justice. Justice is now mine and I go to my husband. As for you, most wicked of all men, let your kinsmen prepare for you a tomb instead of bridal chamber and wedding."

When the Galatian heard these words and felt the poison working, he mounted his chariot hoping that its motion would save him, but soon he had to leave it and get into a litter. And at dusk he died. Camma lived through the night. When she learned that Sinorix had met his end, she died with mind content and spirit joyful.[58]

These are enough examples of Plutarch's delight in stories of woman's courage and constancy, and of his simple narrative of single episodes each with a climax which illustrates his thesis, *mulierum virtutes*.

In Apuleius' novel, tragic, romantic stories appear in which the art of narration is developed to the highest degree. The two most interesting and most elaborately worked out are the stories of the Amorous Stepmother [59]

[58] *Ibid.*, XX.   [59] Apuleius, *Met.* X. 2–12.

and of the Kidnaped Bride Charite.[60]   These will be discussed in the essay on "Apuleius' Art of Story-Telling."

In this review of *Novelle* in classical prose fiction, I may have been tempted to become a *raconteur* rather than a critic.   My object in presenting the stories themselves has been to show by concrete illustration rather than by mere definition what a *Novella* is, to group different types of *Novelle,* and within these groups to suggest precursors of the stories found in the two extant Latin novels.   Traces of primitive taboos and folk-lore appear in stories as remote from each other as Herodotus' tales of Scythia and Sardis, Livy's narrative of the peopling of the Rome of Romulus, and Apuleius' Cupid and Psyche.   The traditional Milesian Tales of Aristides descend to Parthenius and to Apuleius.   Petronius' story of the Woman of Ephesus is a sophisticated version of the Sybaris story or of any local legend, treated realistically and developed by irony into satire.   The prose tragic romance seen in Herodotus, in Xenophon, in Livy, in Plutarch reaches as we shall see its highest peak in Latin literature in Apuleius' story of the Kidnaped Bride Charite with its varied scenes, succession of episodes, prolonged suspense, and intense feeling.   A study of the embryo stories of these types in earlier literature sharpens appreciation of the Latin story-tellers.

The development of the short tale from local legend, single episode or narrative myth to a well-rounded story surcharged with emotion may be seen in its fascinating evolution through the stories themselves.   And a careful study of the technique of narration in *The Metamorphoses* of Apuleius assures us that here is a prince of story-tellers to whom one would still gladly pay an *as* to receive a golden fable.[61]

---

[60] *Ibid.,* IV. 23–27 ; VI. 25–VII. 14 ; VIII. 1–15.   [61] Plin. *Ep.* II. 21, 1.

An American scholar, Dr. B. E. Perry, who has contributed much to the study of the literary technique of the novels by Petronius and Apuleius, has made a chart which represents his own theory of the principal stages in the development of ancient romance.[62]

Comic-unmoral				Serious-idealized
Folk tales (realistic, ironical, or superstitious)		Local legends (heroic)		Popular treatment of historical characters
Romances typified by the "Ονος in which the plots belonged to folklore	Apollonius of Tyre(?)	Pastoral romance of Daphnis and Chloe	Erotic romance of adventure with plots and characters taken mainly from local legend	Romances such as that of Alexander, Belisarius, etc.
Romances with invented plots—the *Satyricon* (?)				
			Erotic romances with invented plots and characters (if any)	

The table as well as his article reveals Dr. Perry's unwillingness to recognize "any progress of development from collections of separate stories or *Schwänke* to novels like that of Petronius." [63]   That is, he omits from his logical line of descent such collections as Parthenius' *Love Romances*, Plutarch's *Mulierum Virtutes,* and Lucian's *Toxaris,* at least *per se* as collections.   And he also leaves out of reckoning for development of form Aristides' *Milesiaca* because there is to his mind no conclusive evidence as to whether they were a collection of stories or a continuous romance as certain critics have tried to prove.   He acknowledges that both Petronius

[62] B. E. Perry, "Petronius and the Comic Romance," in *Class. Phil.* XX (1925), p. 45.
[63] Perry, *ibid.*, p. 41, note 1.

and Apuleius used *Novelle* of a traditional Milesian type and that this recognizable type has links with Ionian stories which appear in Herodotus.[64] So Dr. Perry would certainly admit the influence of separate Oriental *Novelle* in the two Latin novels.

At present we are not concerned with the larger questions of the objects which Petronius and Apuleius had in writing their novels or whether their purposes were one and the same (satire, religious propaganda, entertainment), or with a discussion of all the intricacies and art by which they used their predecessors. This essay has attempted merely to present some of the eastern *Novelle* which are affiliated in type and art with certain *Novelle* used by Petronius and Apuleius. It is hoped that this study will help illuminate a final presentation of the technique of narrative art in the two Latin novels.

[64] B. E. Perry, "An Interpretation of Apuleius' *Metamorphoses*," in *T. P. A. P. A.* LVII (1926), p. 255.

II

LITTLE STORIES IN LATIN ELEGIAC
INSCRIPTIONS

THE very phrase "elegiac inscriptions" transports us to Greek poetry and to those rich garlands of grain, fruit, leaves and flowers festooned through the pages of the Palatine Anthology. From Simonides' crown of glory set over Hellas to the last white violet woven by Meleager into a coronal for his friend, these little Greek elegiacs have been gathered for all time. Types as different as sculptured stele of unknown warrior and carved gem of some beauty in profile, these small poems have taken their place among the supreme works of art of Greece. The greatest of course are those that have grand themes : the national grief over those who fell in the wars with Persia at Thermopylae, Marathon, Salamis. But as moving, on a different scale of emotions, are the Hellenistic epigrams of the little events of every day, of the lives, loves and deaths of those otherwise unremembered. Among them the epitaphs have a peculiar grace from their combination of melancholy and beauty. Few lovers of classical literature have not read over and over their favorites in Mackail's *Select Epigrams of the Greek Anthology*, miniature poems on love, life, death, worship, nature, the family, beauty, change and fate.

No such ancient anthologies of Latin epigrams and

epitaphs are extant. And the modern collection made by Buecheler of the *Carmina Latina Epigraphica* is rarely read except by some young scholar working on a dissertation or some group of students in a seminar. Yet here are collected poems, covering chronologically a period from the early Republic down to Byzantine times, that give invaluable material on the conventions, the reflections and the emotions of the Roman people in the presence of death. Some literary study has been made of them in addition to Buecheler's great work of collection and annotation. Frédéric Plessis and a group of his pupils in *l'école normale supérieure* has published an illuminating edition of selected *Epitaphes*. Edouard Galletier has written as a thesis presented *à la faculté des lettres de Paris* a penetrating and appreciative *Étude sur la poésie funéraire romaine d'après les inscriptions* which must be the basis of all future work. And in English Frank Frost Abbott has left two delightful little sketches on "Literature and the Common People of Rome" in *Society and Politics in Ancient Rome* and "The Poetry of the Common People of Rome" in *The Common People of Ancient Rome*. All these interpretations may tempt readers to pore for themselves over these collected poems which in spite of formulae, ritual and reserve tell so much of Roman ideals and of the *vie intime* of every day.

I have chosen for my own subject of study little stories, or romances, in the elegiac inscriptions. I have limited myself to those written in the elegiac couplet (dactylic hexameter and pentameter) because that meter suited peculiarly as it is to portraying emotion by the alternate flow and ebb of the lines and the halt in the second verse is the most natural verse-vehicle for romantic feeling. I am going to consider two kinds of elegiac inscriptions :

the *graffiti* found in Pompeii and the epitaphs from all over the Roman world.

The sources of these inscriptions are as various as their subjects, and there is great variety too in the objects on which they have been preserved. In Pompeii, they were painted on walls inside rooms of houses or on the outside of houses, shops and public buildings, or they were scratched on walls with the sharp point of some instrument for writing, *stylus* or *graphium*. Elegiac couplets are scrawled all over the walls of the law-court or basilica ; they are found on pillars, on funeral monuments, in houses.

In Rome the inscriptions have been found on as different objects as altar, urn, vault of building, wall of house, wall of catacombs, marble tablet and marble monument to the dead. Many of the epitaphs come from tombs and *columbaria* along the great roads running like arteries out of Rome through all Italy : the Via Appia, Salaria, Nomentana, Aurelia ; and the catacombs have yielded their share. From tombs throughout Italy from Brescia in the north to Beneventum in the south, and from all the provinces of the Roman Empire come these memorials of the dead. Strangely enough, only two of the metrical epitaphs have come from Britain and almost none from Spain, but in Gaul, Sardinia, Dalmatia, and most of all in northern Africa a wealth of material has been discovered. And these provincial inscriptions, which are not written by the natives but by the Roman colonists, with their similarities in theme and coloring to the inscriptions found in the peninsula of Italy, support the monuments in demonstrating the Romanization of the provinces.

There are comparatively few inscriptions extant from the time of the early Republic. Most famous are those from the tomb of the Scipios, those stately epitaphs of great members of a great family of consuls, censors, aediles who added glory to their line. The first to a woman is from the time of the Gracchi, the famous epitaph in iambic senarii on Claudia. Her dignity is as great as that of the Scipio honored in her time [1] and her qualities are those of the ideal Roman matron of the early days : devotion to her husband and sons, care for their home and for the spinning of wool for their robes, and beauty that had secured a fittingly beautiful monument.[2] From the time of the early Empire many inscriptions both pagan and Christian are preserved. The great majority of them are composed for humble people, freedmen and their partners. Taken all together they afford a unique picture of the relations of human beings to each other, the development of the ideal of woman, and the new tenderness for children that grew up in the Empire.

The inscriptions over which I have been poring are those written in the elegiac couplet, composed of a dactylic hexameter and a dactylic pentameter, but I am including among my illustrations also some inscriptions written in irregular combinations of these two lines, hexameter and pentameter. Since the elegiac inscriptions of Pompeii are not sepulchral and make a unique group of comments on the life of one town destroyed at a definite time, I will discuss these first by themselves.

A visitor to Pompeii today as he walks down the newly excavated Street of Abundance is impressed as much by the vividness of the life of the Pompeians as by the horror of their sudden destruction. Here, painted on the walls of buildings on either side of the street are shop signs, cult scenes, election notices. Here is a fuller's establishment with vats all set for dyeing and cleaning. Here is

---

[1] *C.I.L.* I. 38; VI. 1293.　　　　[2] *C.I.L.* I. 1007; VI. 15346.

a wine shop, the pot still on the stove, fantastic goblets in the window, the *amphora* tipped to pour.   Enter some great house-door and you pass through rooms full of color from frescoes on walls and mosaics on floors to garden where new flowers surround old statues, fountains jet upward from old lead pipes, and painted serpents on wall, the genii of the house, protect the home.   Only that skeleton just uncovered in the corner suddenly recalls that not all the members of the family escaped the suffocating fall of pumice-stone on that fatal day in A.D. 79, when Pompeii was destroyed.

The element that most sharply emphasizes this sense of life in the city is the handwriting on the wall, the little verses scratched with sharp instrument on the plaster coating or painted in fresco, spurting out of the life of the common people in a little Campanian town.   Their subjects are legion : election notices, advertisements of lost articles, to-let signs, historical references to siege of Sulla and to battle with the Nucerians, gladiatorial combats, litter of puppies, business dealings, personal records and greetings, love-letters.[3]   Some Pompeian was so impressed by the number of the *graffiti* on the walls of one building, the basilica, or law-court, that he scratched on another couplet about it.

> Strange, O wall, that you have never fallen in ruin,
>   Since you bear a weight, heavy, of many a verse.

> Admiror, paries, te non cecidisse ruina
>   qui tot scriptorum taedia sustineas.[4]

In the election notices a candidate is recommended for office and the names of his supporters are signed.   Such notices are usually in prose, giving the name of the candi-

3 Mau-Kelsey, *Pompeii Its Life and Art,* New York, 1907, pp. 485–508.
4 F. Buecheler, *Carmina Latina Epigraphica,* Leipzig, 1895, 1897, 1926, (*abb.* B.) 957.

date, the office, an exhortation to elect him. Such a notice painted outside a wine shop gives the names of several women, as supporters, evidently gay frequenters of the *thermopolium* : Asellina, Zmyrna (clearly Oriental), Ismurna, Maria (Hebrew).[5] Usually the candidate is mentioned only as "a good man," *v. b.* for *virum bonum,* but once an elegiac couplet commended him.

> If for a life of honor to anyone fame must be granted,
> Surely upon this youth glory must now be bestowed.

> Si qua verecunde viventi gloria danda est,
> huic iuveni debet gloria digna dari.[6]

At the antipodes from this exaltation of virtue is the poster of a wine shop in which a woman whose name was the Greek word for pleasure, Edone, announced :

Here you may drink for a penny.   For two, the wine will be better.
If you will count out four, cup of Falernian quaff.

assibus hic bibitur, dipundium si dederis, meliora bibes,
quattus si dederis, vina Falerna bib(es).[7]

The metrical defects of the first line are obvious.

Many of the elegiac inscriptions are erotic.   A few of these make general comments on love and its effects. One line in faulty meter declares that no one is a fine fellow who has not had a love-affair in his youth.

Nemo est bellus nisi qui amavit mul[ierem] adules[centulus.[8]

Another composed of five pentameters comments on the mutability of the world and woman.

> Nothing on earth can endure.   Time passes ever away.
> Once bright sun has shone, back to the sea it returns.

[5] M. della Corte, *Pompeii, The New Excavations,* Valle di Pompei, 1925, pp. 19–22.
[6] B. 2053.   [7] B. 931.   [8] B. 233.

Soon fair Phoebe must wane.   Full was her orb but just now.
Often too, be assured, Woman's hard cruelty yields.

Nihil durare potest, tempore perpetuo !
Cum bene Sol nituit, redditur Oceano :
Decrescit Phoebe, quae modo plena fuit.
Saepe levis dura fit Venerum feritas ! [9]

Meetings are recorded on the houses where they happened, usually in a prose phrase :

Romula hic cum Staphylo moratur.
Staphylus hic cum Quieta.   (Was it the same Staphylus ?)
[Ba]lbus et Fortuna duo coiuges.

One meeting was honored by a couplet :

In this house once stayed two who were faithful friends.
If you wish our names, Gaius and Aulus they were.

Hic fuimus cari duo nos sine fine sodales.
Nomina si [quaeris, Caius et Aulus erant.[10]

Greetings in the form of letters are inscribed on the walls as though the writing down would by some magic convey them to the absent.   One in prose is longer than most of them.

Hirtia Psacas always and everywhere sends good wishes to Gaius Hostilius Conops, her husband, guide and wise adviser, to her brother and her sister Diodota and her brother Fortunatus and Celer, and to her Primigenia.[11]

Messages to the absent in elegiac couplets are more colored by emotion and more fanciful.   Amor dictates one letter.

Love gives me words as I write and Cupid is ever my prompter.
Now may I die if I wish God to be called without thee.

Scribenti mi dictat Amor mostratque Cupido :
a] peream, sine te si deus esse velim.[12]

9 della Corte, *op. cit.*, p. 80.   10 B. 2055.
11 *C. I. L.* IV. Suppl. II. 3905.   12 B. 937.

Another celebrates the beauty of a little lady.

Let one who has not seen the Venus Apelles painted
  Look at my Dolly and think : "Such was the goddess of love."

Si quis non vidi(t) Venerem, quam pin[xit Apelles,
  pupa(m) mea(m) aspiciat : talis et [illa nitet.[13]

One takes the form of a wish, with a touch of irony at the end.

This is my prayer for Sabina : that always her beauty may flower.
  Always may she be fair.   Long may she still be a maid.

Sic tibi contingat semper florere, Sabina,
  contingat forma(e) sisque puella diu.[14]

With these messages on the walls of Pompeii, I will include two *graffiti* found on the Palatine in Rome. One is a declaration of fidelity.

If there is faith in man, I swear I have loved you only
  From that day when first each to the other was known.

Siqua fides hominum est, unam te semper amavi,
  ex quo notities inter utrosque fuit.[15]

The other is a description of the torment of love.

Strength in my soul there is none, and sleep never closes my eyelids.
  All night long and all day surges the sea of my love.

Vis] nulla est animi, non somnus claudit ocellos,
  noctes [atque] dies aestuat omnis amor.[16]

The longest letter inscribed on a wall at Pompeii is one found in the "House of the Doctor," written in eight irregular verses, with a suggestion of an attempt at elegiacs. It is the most emotional and unrestrained of all these *graffiti* messages. I translate in elegiac couplets.

Oh !   If 'twere only my right with my arm round your neck to enfold you,

[13] B. 2057.   [14] B. 2059.   [15] B. 939.   [16] B. 943.

Then on your tender lips tenderest kisses to press !
Go now, my dear little girl, entrust to the winds your caresses.
 'Las and alack, my dear.   Light is the nature of man.
Oft when I lay awake as the midnight hour was passing,
  Often I thought to myself : Those whom once Fortune exalts,
Those same men she casts down, in a moment she topples them
    over.
So when Venus has joined suddenly bodies of men,
Dawn parts lovers again, or a wall.   And what then ?   Ah !
    Love !

O utinam liceat collo complexa tenere
  braciola et teneris oscula ferre labelis.
i nunc, ventis tua gaudia, pupula, crede.
crede mihi, levis est natura virorum.
saepe ego cu(m) media vigilare(m) perdita nocte
haec mecum medita(n)s : multos Fortuna quos supstulit alte,
  hoc modo proiectos subito praecipitesque premit ;
sic Venus ut subito coiunxit corpora amantum,
  dividit lux, et se paries quid, ama.[17]

The exhortation in that last categorical imperative
ama leads on to another group of poems which contain
advice.   Several are directed to those who seek to injure
or to hinder love.

Let him chain the winds who seeks to upbraid true lovers.
  Let that man forbid flow of perennial spring.

Alliget hic auras, si quis obiurgat amantes,
  et vetet assiduas currere fontis aquas.[18]

Some are more personal and violent.

If any rival by chance desires to harm my lady,
  On lone mountain peaks may he be scorched by his love.

Si quis forte meam cupiet vio[lare] puellam,
  illum in desertis montibus urat amor.[19]

A similar imprecation found in Rome changes the
curse on the rival to a hope that on remote mountains a
bear may devour him.[20]

---

[17] B. 950.   [18] B. 944.   [19] B. 953.   [20] B. 954.

A denunciation of venality appears in lyric form.

Once I have written my Love and the Lady has read, she is mine.
  Once she has named her price, she is not mine, but the world's.

Quoi scripsi semel et legit, mea iure puellast :
  quae pretium dixit, non mea sed populi est.[21]

Five which begin with the same phrase *quisquis amat*
contain advice to lovers.

Blessed be the man who loves and cursed be the man who will not
    love,
  But twice cursed be one who has impeded the game.

Quis]quis amat valeat, pereat qui nescit amare,
  bis tanto pereat quis quis amare vetat.[22]

The next contains a familiar proverb.

A man who's in love should never bathe in the springs that are hot.
  Child and adult once burned always must dread a new flame.

Quisquis amat, calidis non debet fontibus uti,
  nam nemo flammas ustus amare potest.[23]

A strange bit of folklore, that mulberries are an aphro-
disiac, seems to be referred to in the following couplet.
The literal translation of the last line, "I gladly eat mulberries," has been modified.

One who loves dark lady is burning with dead black coals.
  When I see dark girl, tonic I take for my heart.

Quisquis amat nigra(m), nigris carbonibus ardet;
  nigra(m) cum video, mora libenter aedeo.[24]

The next which is very fanciful I have translated in
a lighter meter than the Latin elegiacs. It pictures a
lover's bold assault on an offending goddess.

[21] B. 942.   [22] B. 945; 946.   [23] B. 948.   [24] B. 2056.

Now, Lovers, come.   For I am bound
    To crush Dame Venus' frame.
With cudgel stout and right arm sound,
    A smacking blow I'll aim.
If she can break my tender heart,
    Why, Lovers, tell me pray,
With cudgel cannot I make smart
    The goddess' head today ?

Quisquis amat, veniat.   Veneri volo frangere costas
    fustibus et lumbos debilitare deae.
Si potest illa mihi tenerum pertundere pectus,
    quit ego non possim caput i[ll]ae frangere fuste ? [25]

Next this whimsical little gem, I will place a poem of
two and a half couplets that is inspired with real emotion,
sincere, however ephemeral.

Why do you postpone joys when only the will is lacking ?
    Why exalt fond hope ?   Why for tomorrow delay ?
So you will force to die the one who perforce lives without you.
    Death will be a gift.   Not to be tortured a boon.
Yet what hope has filched, hope still returns to a lover.

Si potes et non vis, cur gaudia differs
    spemque foves et cras usque redire iubes ?
er]go coge mori quem sine te vivere cogis :
    munus erit, certe non cruciasse boni.
quod spes eripuit, spes certe redd[i]t amanti. [26]

In spite of the mistakes in meter, the feeling in these
lines made such an appeal that passers-by wrote under
the poem their approval and sympathy.

May one who reads this never read another verse again.

qui hoc leget, nuncquam posteac aliud legat.

A second added in prose:

May the writer of the above never know safety.

numquam sit salvos qui supra scripsit.

And two others commented : "You speak the truth,"
vere dicis, and "Good luck, Hedystus," *Hedysto feliciter.*

[25] B. 947.   [26] B. 949.

Very different in their flippant irony are three couplets about etiquette painted on three walls of a dining room in the house of Epidius Hymenaeus.

Water to wash the feet, and a slave-boy to rub down the sweaty.
  Now a clean throw on the couch. Hands off my napkins, my
  friend.

Not a flirtatious glance and never a drooping eyelid
  Cast on another's wife. Honor must hold here, my friend.

Use here gracious words and postpone hideous quarrelling
  If you can, and if not, kindly depart to your home.

Abluat unda pedes, puer et detergeat udos :
  mappa torum velet, lintea nostra cave.

Lascivos voltus et blandos aufer ocellos
  coniuge ab alterius, sit tibi in ore pudor.

Utere blanditiis] odiosaque iurgia differ,
  si potes, aut gressus ad tua tecta refer.[27]

The sprightly gaiety of these couplets in a dining room finds an echo in the ironic generalization on a funeral monument in Rome.

Bathing and drinking and loving : these are what shatter our
  bodies.
  Yet life is just that : bathing and drinking and love.

Balnea vina Venus corrumpunt corpora nostra,
  set vitam faciunt b(alnea) v(ina) V(enus).[28]

Very different from such *graffiti,* full of life's fitful fever and little ironies, are the epitaphs of the dead. Many a *memento mori* is tinged with a melancholy gravity. Joy is forever bidding adieu. And when real feeling forces a way through formulae and ritual, it is clad in sable robes. Stoic resignation sets lips firmly. And the Epicureanism of some of the tombstones seems bravado in face of a spectre.

[27] B. 2054 ; della Corte, *op. cit.,* p. 61.   [28] B. 1499.

A first reading of hundreds of these funereal inscriptions gives an impression of sameness because of the repeated formulae. Certain phrases occur so often that a theory has been advanced by M. Cagnat that manuals of epitaphs must have been in the hands of the stonecutters from which selections were made for individual monuments.[29] The engravers often mutilated their models from ignorance or in adapting them to the needs of their clients or in introducing proper names. An example of such formulae as these manuals may have contained is

$$
\text{Te} \left\{ \begin{array}{l} \text{lapis} \\ \text{terra} \end{array} \right\} \text{obtestor} \left\{ \begin{array}{l} \text{levis ut} \\ \text{leviter} \end{array} \right\} \text{super ossa} \left\{ \begin{array}{l} \text{residas} \\ \text{quiescas} \end{array} \right\}
$$

$$
\text{Et} \left\{ \begin{array}{l} \text{tenerae} \\ \text{florenti} \\ \text{mediae} \end{array} \right\} \text{aetati ne gravis esse velis.}
$$

This theory is strengthened by Friedländer's belief in regard to the sculptured sarcophagi : that they were for the most part not made for special orders, but executed in advance and offered in the shops for the choice of the purchaser. Focillon, whose comments I have been quoting, thinks that perhaps, even if there were not a manual of inscriptions, the stonecutters had a number of epitaphs drawn up to offer as a choice.[30]   Galletier, who contests Cagnat's theory of a manual of formulae for the stonecutters, thinks that imitations and copies of inscriptions were made by the authors of the epitaphs and that possibly in course of time anthologies of met-

---

[29] R. Cagnat, "Sur les manuels professionnels des graveurs, d'inscriptions romaines," in *Rev. de Phil.* vol. XIII (1889), pp. 51–65.

[30] See H. Focillon, "Étude sur la Poésie funéraire à Rome d'après les Inscriptions," in F. Plessis, *Poésie latine, Epitaphes,* pp. xv–lx.

rical epitaphs were made which were used by the authors
for models.[31]

In this general introduction to the study of the elegiac
epitaphs, I am drawing largely on Galletier's admirable
thesis (now out of print), and I wish once for all to ac-
knowledge my debt to his exhaustive and penetrating
study.

Certain conventions in the framework and design of
the funereal inscriptions existed as well as the formulae.
Often a *praescriptum* in prose preceded the metrical
epitaph. It began with D. M. (*dis manibus*) and contained the triple name of the dead, his parentage, his
age. As the name was an essential feature of a memorial
and the complete name could hardly be given in a short
poem which used generally only one *nomen* (the *gen-
tilicium* or the *cognomen*) the prose inscription usually
carried the full name, and sometimes too the names of
the parents, the name of the *gens* and the place of birth.
The date of death unfortunately is not given. Often
after the little poem a prose *subscriptum* followed which
might contain the same material which the *praescriptum*
sometimes gave. In some cases *praescriptum* and *subscriptum* stood on either side of the metrical epitaph.

Another conventional feature of the inscription is an
appeal to the passer-by to stop and read. Some of these
appeals are very curt, some are couched with elaborate
politeness. The ingenuity of the poet comes out in variations of the appeal. A short statement about the life,
the virtues and the characteristics of the dead was then
introduced. And finally at the end, the dead man
thanks the passer-by for stopping and wishes him well.

---

[31] E. Galletier, *Étude sur la Poésie funéraire romaine d'après les Inscriptions*. Thèse présentée à la faculté des lettres de Paris, Paris, 1922.

Such was the brief form of the epitaphs of the second and
first centuries B.C.   Toward the end of the Republic this
conciseness and brevity disappeared and the central part
of the poem, the biographical lines and the lamentation,
developed until the inscription resembled an elegiac
poem rather than an epigram.[32]

In this expansion of the central part of the inscription,
the dramatic character which the simple epitaphs had
already assumed in the address to the passer-by was developed from this embryo to full-fledged dialogue.   At
first the epitaphs give a description of the person lauded,
in the third person.   Then a speaker appears who talks
in the first person.   And this speaker is sometimes a
living character who speaks to the dead or about the
dead.   Usually it is a husband who addresses his dead
wife or praises her.   In other epitaphs, the dead speaks
to the living, and here most often a wife speaks, lament-
ing her separation from her husband, or her desertion of
her children.   Once a baby girl who died when she was
a year old speaks for herself.   Other epitaphs use a combination of a description of the dead in the third person
and direct address.   In others the dead speaks to different persons.   Eventually dialogue develops between the
dead and the living.   On one tombstone four different
speakers are given words.   There are many dialogues in
the Palatine Anthology so that this use of it in the Latin
inscriptions may be due in part to the Greek, but it
grows naturally out of inner feeling and longing to hold
converse with the lost.

Galletier discusses the authorship of the epitaphs as
well as their plan.[33]   Some are clearly written by the individuals who speak, for example, the one in which Pub-

32 See E. Galletier, *op. cit.*, p. 221.
33 E. Galletier, *op. cit.*, pp. 237-43.

licius says he dictated the epitaph.[34] There were grammarians capable of writing a literary epitaph, for Blaesianus Biturix could compose his own by making a neat combination of lines from Lucretius and Vergil.[35] There are also literary inscriptions known to be written by great poets, Naevius, Pacuvius, Ennius, and there are others by minor poets who describe themselves and their works.[36] In the case of great persons, the metrical epitaphs must have been written by members of these highly educated families. For humble persons the question of authorship is more difficult. Some state that a father has composed an epitaph for his son,[37] or a soldier for his comrade and friend.[38] And the very character of some of these inscriptions, their simplicity, their poverty of thought, their mistakes, suggests that the humble persons themselves wrote them. And many of them are virtually signed documents in which the poet acknowledges his creation.[39] Certainly the *graffiti* at Pompeii come from the people and prove their ability to write verses.

The earliest inscriptions are dry and formal, much like the inscriptions on the bases of statues. Fuller poetical inscriptions begin in the last years of the Republic with the political and social advance of the plebeians and the individualism developed by the civil wars. But with a few exceptions, the metrical epitaph remained an epigram nearly to the Christian era and was characterized by conciseness and brevity. Such epitaphs continued to be written by persons of taste down through the history of Latinity.

In the Augustan Age epigraphical poetry was enriched

[34] B. 479 (Tusculum, in defective hexameters).
[35] B. 481 (in hexameters. Cf. Lucret. IV. 451 and Verg. *Aen.* VIII. 349).
[36] B. 1111, 1248, 1250, 1251.   [37] B. 521, 607.
[38] B. 1099.   [39] B. 1191, 1192, 1237.

by contact with a new literary type, the ἐπικήδειον (later
called θρῆνος), a chant of grief recited in the presence of
the dead. It was partly a lament, partly a laudation.
This form developed in the Alexandrian Age. We
know that Aratus, Euphorion and Parthenius composed
such poems. Among the Romans Calvus wrote one
(now lost) for his wife, Quintilia, Catullus his *ave atque
vale* for his brother, Propertius *epicedia* for the soldier
Gallus, Petus, Marcellus and Cornelia, Ovid for Tibullus, Albinovanus Celsus and Augustus. This new genre
undoubtedly helped develop the long epitaph with its
fuller expression of emotion, its many details, its mythological coloring, its pictures of the lower world, and its
apostrophes to the dead, to fate, to mother earth, to the
muses. And as the philosophical consolation developed
from the *epicedion,* so philosophical reflections and
moral advice come to find their place in the Latin
epitaph. With the advent of Christianity, the consolations of the faith appeared side by side with Stoic
fortitude and Epicurean scepticism about a future
world.

The Christian metrical inscriptions were very popular.
They were composed by Pope Damasus and S.S. Am-
brosius, Hieronymus, Sidonius and Fortunatus. They
were written not only about bishops, priests and martyrs,
but for the faithful in humble life. They differ little
from the pagan inscriptions of the same date. They are
usually rather long. The ornamentation and decorative
motifs of the sarcophagi are the same as the pagan ones :
Genii, Amors and Psyches, the Dioscuri, the mask of
Medusa, doves picking fruit. The praise of the dead,
the philosophical reflections, even the references to the
mythology of the lower world all resemble those of the

pagan inscriptions. In one epitaph the phrase *summi rector Olimpi* is used for Christ.[40] It was thus that in the Christian poetry down to the end of the seventh century the metrical epitaph born two centuries before Christ survived.

The language of the Latin metrical inscriptions is a curious mixture of vulgar speech, the *sermo cotidianus* with all its obscurities and mistakes, and a poetic diction arising first from imitation then from genuine feeling. With these two styles, the familiar and the literary, appear incongruous combinations of banalities and imaginative flights. Puns, riddles, acrostics nudge elbows with flowerlike half-lines from Vergil. In many of the poems beautiful quotations are poorly assimilated with the author's own paucity of ideas and bad taste. But in others genuine feeling, finding its models in great elegiacs, expresses itself in almost a new poetry of lamentation for the dead.

The use of the poets in the inscriptions varies from direct quotation,[41] to quotation in solution, *cento* made up of many quotations from different authors, and more general influence. The tables at the end of each of Buecheler's two volumes of the *Carmina Latina Epigraphica* show the vast use of the poets in the epitaphs. There are reminiscences and quotations of Lucretius, Horace, the elegiac poets, Statius, Lucan and Martial, but most of all Vergil and Ovid are used. As is natural from the verse form, often a vague, general influence of Catullus, Tibullus and Propertius appears. And some of the long epitaphs of the Empire which approach the form and style of the *epicedion* are actual mosaics of lines and half-lines cut out of many poets. This general use of the

[40] B. 770.   [41] B. 1786 (*Aen.* I. 607-9).

Latin poets attests the education of the freedmen and
freedwomen who wrote the majority of the poems.

After this long introductory account of the Latin
elegiac inscriptions we are ready to study the poems
themselves.   How many lines of approach to them there
are may be seen from the table of contents of Galletier's
study : the religious and philosophical value of the
epitaphs ; their historical value for biography, for family
life, for social life ; their literary value.   My own present
interest in them is that they are a source-book for the
study of human relations in a class of people who have
hardly found voice in other forms of literature — the
freedmen, the common people of ancient Rome.   From
their tombs they tell for themselves something of their
vie intime and of their regard for their women and children.   Out of vast numbers I have selected those that
recount episodes, throw light on character or illuminate
personal relations.   Inevitably they are almost all poems
about women.

Their beautiful names run through the verses like
musical motifs : Latin names, Anna, Argentea (the Silver
Lady), Florentina (Lady of Flowers), Fabia Fuscinilla,
Helvia, Probina (the Noble), Serena (the Calm), Tur-
tina (the Dove) ; Greek names, Euphrosyne (Joy), Helpis
(Hope), Homonoea (Harmony), Lalema (the Prattler),
Philematium (Little Kiss), Rhodine (Flower of the Rose),
Glypte, Lesbia.   The authors of the epitaphs liked to
linger over the names and comment on their sweet sound
or prolong their dear meaning.

> Glypte, sweet name, lies here.
>
> Dulce istic nomen Glypte iacet.[42]
>
> Flavia Nicopolis, nomen dulce tuum,[43]

[42]. B. 1307.   [43] B. 1184.

has her lovely long name used twice in her epitaph. Flavia Amoena is said to be *ut rosa amoena*.[44] Rhodine, Lady of the Roses, is said to have died in the very flower of her youth, as her brief crimson gleam vanished.[45] Of Argentea, the Silver Lady, it is said that mother and child bore the same sweet name.[46] And Turtina was called dove in nature as in name.[47]

Of such passing fairness, the rose is the natural symbol. But in one epitaph of linked sweetness long drawn out Titus Aelius Stephanus, freedman of Augustus, plants a garden of flowers for Flavia Nicopolis.[48]

Oh ! If the gods above would only grant to my asking
　That I might see from your mound many a new flower spring,
Verdant branch, amaranth, red rose, and the violet shining !
　So some passer-by halting might tarry a while,
Gaze at the flowers and read these verses written above you,
　Then think : "Here now blooms Flavia Nicopolis."

O mihi si superi vellent praestare roganti
　ut tuo de tumulo flos ego cerna novum
crescere vel viridi ramo vel flore amaranti
vel roseo vel purpureo violaeque nitore,
ut qui praeteriens gressu tardante viator
videret hos flores, titulum legat et sibi dicat
　'hoc flos est corpus Flaviae Nicopolis.'

The adjectives used in describing these dear dead women show the ideals and traits developed in their times. In the Republican epitaph of Aurelia Philematium the wife declares that she was

Chaste, pure, unknown to the crowd, true to my husband alway,

Casta, pudens, volgei nescia, feida viro.[49]

This old ideal of the *Hausfrau* persisted down through the empire, and pagan and Christian inscriptions honor the same virtues. Sempronia of the second century was

---

[44] B. 967.　　　[45] B. 1431.　　　[46] B. 1336.　　　[47] B. 2103.
[48] B. 1184. (The meter is irregular.)　　　[49] *C. I. L.* I. 1011.

dulcis, casta viro, reverens pia kara fidelis,[50]

and a Christian wife was addressed as

casta, decus morum, sapiens, devota marito.[51]

The wife is praised for her efforts to please her husband [52] and her *obsequium*.   Later, beginning in the first
century B.C., a new type of woman developed, whose
talents, graces, and beauty are celebrated.   Eucharis, a
little dancer of the middle of the first century, was called

docta, erodita paene Musarum manu,[53]

Euphrosyne was *docta* and *formosa*.[54]   On the tomb of
Pedana her lover who wrote her epitaph had her lyre
carved.[55]   And like Pedana, Sabis was docta lyra.[56]
Glypte was witty and gay in conversation.[57]   Galletier
comments that none of these inscriptions about accom-
plished women come from the provinces, but there the
old ideal of woman persisted.[58]   A new ideal of woman
appears on some of the Christian monuments, where the
philanthropy of the dead person is mentioned and she
is called the mother of the poor, *mater egentum*.[59]

Few facts are told about the women who are so lauded,
and the themes of the inscriptions are few.   The main
one is the happiness of married life, and either the length
of its endurance is celebrated or its brevity is regretted.
Even when allowance is made for the exaggeration which
is an essential feature of epitaphs, it seems clear that the
deterioration of the marriage tie which was conspicuous
among the Roman aristocracy in later Republic and
early Empire was not known to the humble.   Epithets
of wives often recurring on the tombs are *uniiuga* and
univira.   Some inscriptions record years of harmonious

---

[50] B. 1192.   [51] B. 1430.   [52] B. 1030, 1440, 1033.
[53] B. 55, 9 (in senarii).   [54] B. 1136.   [55] B. 1301.   [56] B. 1302.
[57] B. 1307.   [58] Galletier, *op. cit.*, p. 129.   [59] B. 1434.

life together.[60]   In course of time, in the middle and
lower classes, marriage became more and more a union
of two intelligent people, who worked together for the
interests of their home.   One husband assured his wife,
Florentina, that while he was busy with his military
career, his mind was free from all anxiety about the house
because of her wise management.[61]   The long story told
in the famous prose inscription known as the *laudatio
Turiae* gives a vivid and thrilling account of how one
lady protected her husband's interest during the civil
war.[62]   The names of the pair were probably Turia and
Q. Lucretius Vespillo.   While Lucretius was away with
Pompey's army in the war, Turia's parents were both
murdered.   She seems to have discovered the criminals
and brought them to justice.   She kept Lucretius sup-
plied in his absence with money and provisions.   When
relatives contested her father's will which left his property jointly to her husband and herself, she did not permit them to alter these conditions and oust her husband
from joint control of the inheritance.   When after
Caesar's death and the foundation of the second triumvirate, her husband's name was on the list of proscribed,
she hid him in their home between the roof and the
ceiling of one of the bedrooms until Octavian granted
him pardon.   In the peace of the following years, she
again showed her character by urging her husband to
divorce her and marry again, since she was childless and
she wished his family perpetuated.   Lucretius rejected
this proposal with horror because of his devotion to his
wife and his happiness with her.   His character sketch
of her presents again the old ideal of the Roman matron,

[60] B. 960, 5–6.   [61] B. 1429, 5–6.
[62] *C. I. L.* VI. 1527 ; W. Warde Fowler, *Social Life at Rome in the Age of
Cicero*, New York, 1920, pp. 158–67.

though Turia is one of the best illustrations of the development of her character in the late Republic.

"You were a faithful wife to me — and an obedient one : you were kind and gracious, sociable and friendly : you were assiduous at your spinning : you followed the religious rites of your family and your state, and admitted no foreign cults or degraded magic. You did not dress conspicuously, nor seek to make a display in your household arrangements.   Your duty to our whole household was exemplary : you tended my mother as carefully as if she had been your own.   You had innumerable other excellences, in common with all other worthy matrons, but these I have mentioned were peculiarly yours." [63]

This inscription and many others beside showing woman's practical helpfulness and intelligence give touching pictures of conjugal fidelity and happiness.

Take me, husband dearest, to share thy tomb with thee always,
    For it is death indeed not to find death with thyself.
Here all my mind lies buried and here lies buried my lifeblood.
    Hence to endure thy death always is death to myself.

Suscipe me sociam tumulis dulciss [ime coniux,
    cum mors est tecum non meruis [se mori.
hic mea mens simul est, simul hic mea [vita sepulta,
    mortem ferre tuam mors mihi [semper erit.[64]

A quieter sorrow is expressed in a couplet to a passer-by.

Envious man, why rejoice ?   This woman now dead shall live for
    me.
    Always in my eyes golden her memory be.

Invide, quid gaudes ?   illa hic mihi mortua vivet,
    illa meis oculis aurea semper erit.[65]

Another is filled with a serene faith.

Julius and Trebia lived together through many and long years.
    This their union remains : marriage eternal is theirs.

63 W. W. Fowler's translation, *op. cit.*, pp. 166–67.
64 B. 1338, 1–4.   65 B. 1298.

Iulius cum Trebia bene vixit multosq. per annos
   coniugio aeterno hic quoque nunc remanet.[66]

There is a moving appeal to Mother Earth who touches
her children with a mother's tenderness, to rest lightly
on Fortunata.[67]   In some inscriptions a poor man laments that he can set up only a poor little memorial to
his dear wife because of his poverty.[68]

Very few episodes stand out among these expressions
of feeling.   A little dancer not yet eight years old danced
on dainty feet down the last road just as she was beginning to practice her merry art of wantonness.[69]   A young
woman seems to have been killed by robbers for her
jewelry.[70]   Another records in her epitaph that she is
not to be mourned for she belonged to Orbius Natalis
and was the seventh one whom he loved.[71] · The most
common fatality mentioned is death in childbirth, often
with the baby.

Several epitaphs are poems of exile, tinged with home-
sickness.   One found in Carthage in the burial place of
the retinue of Caesar (time of the Antonines), though
its form is a tasteless acrostic, raises a real lament for
Prima whose fate it was to die in Libya though she was
born in Rome.[72]   A Pontia followed her husband, oppressed by fate and hatred, to Corsica.[73]   Helpis, a young
Christian of Sicily, was driven by love of her husband
far from her native land, but now rests before the throne
of the eternal judge, no longer an exile.[74]   Another
young woman who had followed her devoted husband
through the Sporades and the Gauls had to die when
her second child was born.[75]   The very simplicity of

---

[66] B. 1325. [67] B. 1039. [68] B. 1042, 2113.
[69] B. 1166. [70] B. 1037.
[71] B. 1032.   See Buecheler's notes and Plessis, *op. cit.*, pp. 172–75, for different
interpretations.
[72] B. 1187.   [73] B. 1846.   [74] B. 1432.   [75] B. 2080.

the statement of such facts increases their poignancy.

The epitaphs of Pomptilla tell more elaborately the same story.   They were found in Cagliari, Sardinia, on the walls of a great rock-cut tomb of several rooms with an entrance façade decorated like a temple.   There are seven Latin inscriptions and seven Greek inscriptions which either in dactylic hexameters or elegiac couplets commemorate Atilia Pomptilla, wife of Philippus.[76] The date of the tomb seems to be the early part of the second century.

Nothing is known of Pomptilla and Philippus except what the epitaphs tell.   Philippus had been exiled from Rome to Sardinia and his wife, Pomptilla, followed him. Once when in an illness she saw that her husband was in danger of death, she begged the gods to let her give her life in exchange for her husband's as Alcestis did for Admetus.   Their union lasted forty-two years.   Kaibel suggests that in the leisure of his exile Philippus had time to write these numerous epitaphs which lament and exalt his wife.   Over and over he repeats in two languages the same theme with slight variations : Pomptilla gave her life for mine.   The first four will give an idea of the sequence.

A

Child of great Rome am I, Atilia, love of Philippus,
Sharer of his sad fate as I followed him here to this land.
Here now enshrined am I by the tender hands of my husband,
For whose life I prayed the gods to take toll of my own.
Kind were the gods, and do thou, O Fame, grant the fame that I
    merit.

Urbis alumna, graves casus huc usque secuta
coniugis infelicis, Atilia, cura Philippi,
hic sita sum manibus gratis sacrata mariti,

---

pro cuius vita vitam pensare precanti
indulsere dei.   ne cesses, fama : meremur.

B

Passer, no temple is this though often here thou hast worshipped.
  This small house confines ashes and bones of a wife.
I who followed my husband lie buried in Sardoan country
  And fame says that I wished only to die for my lord.

Quod credis templum, quod saepe viator adoras,
  Pomptillae cineres ossaq. parva tegit.
Sardoa tellure premor comitata maritum,
  proq. viro fama est me voluisse mori.

C

Forty-one years we lived together in love unbroken.
  One faith gave to us both joys that can never be told.
And Pomptilla before she crossed the waters of Lethe,
  Said to me : "Husband, O live !   Take all my days, O my lord !"
Now eternal peace and the silence of gloomy Pluto
  For them both have built home in a tomb for their love.

Unu et viginti bis iuncti vix[i]mus annos,
  una fides nobis gaudia multa dedit.
et prior at Lethen cum sit Pompti[ll]a recepta,
  'tempore tu' dixit 'vive, Philippe, m[e]o.'
nunc aeterna quies Ditisq. silentia maesti
  hanc statuere ambis pro pietate domum.

D

While Pomptilla was sadly bewailing her suffering husband,
  Vow made she to die giving herself for her lord.
Straightway she seemed to escape to the peaceful, ultimate quiet.
  Dead, my wife was dead !   Gods, ye who granted her prayer,
Swift, ah ! too swift were ye then to fulfill a vow for another,
  Saving the life of a man, letting his darling depart.

Languentem tristis dum flet Pomptilla maritum,
  vovit pro vita coniugis ipsa mori.
pro[t]inus in placidam delabi visa quietem
  occidit.   o celere[s] at mala vota dei,

has audire preces, vitam servare [marito,
  ut pereat vita dulcior illa m[ihi.

An embryo dialogue exists in these epitaphs of Pomptilla as Atilia Pomptilla speaks in A, Philippus speaks in
the first person in B, C, D, and in C a speech of Pomptilla
to her husband is quoted. Other inscriptions have a
much more complete and striking use of this dramatic
device. In several two-part poems there are two speakers but they do not talk directly to each other. In the
Republican epitaph of Philematium the first part, A,
consists of seven lines (one pentameter is lost) spoken by
Philematium herself about herself and her husband.
In part B (four lines) her husband talks about Philematium. Both poems are full of deep but restrained feeling.[77] Another longer epitaph found in Madaura has
two parts, the first in elegiac couplets addressed to a
hospes, the second in hexameters addressed to a *viator.*
In the first the virtues of Mammosa and the grief of her
husband are described ; in the second, her husband,
Florus, is honored by their three children. Both parts
are written in the third person, with dignity and for-
mality, and Mammosa's old-time virtues are exalted.[78]
A third two-part poem of another type written in various
meters is all spoken by a little boy of twelve who addresses his playmates first, begging their pity for his early
death, and then, in two lines, talks to his mother urging
her not to grieve since this had to be ; it was the will of
his Fate.[79]

Real dialogue, or conversation between two people, appears in both short and long poems. In one, a wife
speaks a couplet to her dead husband, then he responds
in a second. I have tried in my translation to express

[77] B. 959.   [78] B. 2107.   [79] B. 1537.

the simple feeling. I could not preserve the rhetorical balance of the two couplets with the contrasts of *servavi* and *ornasti, coniux* and *uxor* coming at the same points in the lines, or the subtle contrast of meaning between *manes* and *inferias*.

A

Dearest husband, for you the wedding chamber I guarded.
Now must I guard here for you, tomb instead of a couch.

B

Honor to me you have offered by tears, O pitiful woman,
Wrong it were for the shades ever to crave other boon.

A

Servavi thalamum genio, dulcissime coniux :
    servandus nunc est pro thalamo tumulus.

B

Ornasti et manes lacrimis, miserabilis uxor :
    haud optare alias fas erat inferias.[80]

In another epitaph of two couplets, the living husband whose name was, I think, Hardalio, speaks to the dead wife who then replies.

Fortunata you were, chaste, pure, rare prize for a husband.
    This is my tribute to you. So does Hardalio please ?

Rightly named am I, because, my dear, you survive me ;
    You being safe, I live, blessed in the sons of my sons.

Casta bona inviolans, rarum hoc á coniuge munus,
    Fortunata, tibi. Sic placet Hardalio ?

[80] B. 1139.

Nomine digna meo, quod tu mihi, ka[r]e, superstes,
  natorum natis te incolumi vigui.[81]

The longest of these elegiac dialogues comes from an
elegant marble *cippus,* found in Rome, which commem-
orates Claudia Homonoea, wife of Atimetus Anteroti-
anus, a freedman, son of Pamphilus, a freedman of Tiberius Caesar Augustus. As stately as the long prose
praescriptum in Latin and Greek are the twenty-six
elegiac lines of the metrical inscription. There are three
speakers, but each part is a dialogue : in A the dead wife
speaks to a passer-by who responds in a couplet ; in B
the husband speaks (six lines) to his dead wife who makes
a speech of eight lines in reply. Homonoea first begs
the traveler to halt and give ear. She then utters her
own laudation and declares that her sorrow over her
early death was caused only by her husband's grief. The
traveler gives the conventional good wish and declares
she was worthy of life's blessings.

Atimetus declares that he would gladly have offered
his life for hers and since he could not do that, he will
at least follow her. Homonoea at once forbids his
suicide, preaches resignation to fate and begs him not to
shatter his youth with tears that avail naught, but to take
up life again. A fine elegance of expression and the few
mythological allusions clothe very poignant feeling.

A

Homonoea   You who advance care-free, I beg you, tarry a little.
speaks: Few are the words I will speak, I, Homonoea, now
               dead.
            I who in life outshone all brilliant ladies now lie here.
               Small is my tomb though to me Venus had granted
               her form,
            Pallas had taught me her arts and the Graces had given
               me beauty.

[81] B. 1289.

Yet on my nineteen years fate laid her envious hands.
Not for myself I make moan, for sadder than death is
the sorrow
Atimetus my own feels for the loss of his wife.

The passer- Light be the earth upon you, O lady, worthy of living,
by speaks: Worthy of all the boons given you once by the gods.

B

Atimetus If by the cruel fate lives might be weighed in the bal-
speaks: ance,
Safety be given a friend, balancing life against life,
All the rest of my days I would cast in the scales for you,
loved one.
Dear Homonoea, for you gladly I'd weigh out my
soul.
Now I will do what I can : I will flee from the light and
the great gods.
You will I seek o'er the Styx, following you by my
death.

Homonoea Cease, my husband, to shatter your youth by piteous
speaks: weeping,
And to disturb my fate, grieving o'er what has been
lost.
Nothing avail these tears and the fates no mortal can
alter.
We have lived and all come to this end at the last.
Cease, and never again may you feel the pain of this
moment.
Now may all the gods turn friendly ears to your
prayers.
All my youth that death cut off from me prematurely,
All now be yours to live.   You now must live for us
both.

A

Tu qui secura procedis mente, parumper
siste gradum quaeso verbaque pauca lege.
illa ego quae claris fueram praelata puellis,
hoc Homonoea brevi condita sum tumulo,
cui formam Paphie, Charites tribuere decorem,
quam Pallas cunctis artibus erudiit.

nondum bis denos aetas mea viderat annos,
    iniecere manus invida fata mihi.
nec pro me queror hoc, morte est mihi tristior ipsa
    maeror Atimeti coniugis ille mei.
'sit tibi terra levis, mulier dignissima vita
    quaeque tuis olim perfruerere bonis.'

B

Si pensare animas sinerent crudelia fata
    et posset redimi morte aliena salus,
quantulacumque meae debentur tempora vitae,
    pensassem pro te, cara Homonoea, libens.
at nunc quod possum, fugiam lucemque deosque,
    ut te matura per Styga morte sequar.
'parce tuam, coniux, fletu quassare iuventam
    fataque maerendo sollicitare mea.
nil prosunt lacrimae nec possunt fata moveri.
    viximus, hic omnis exitus unus habet.
parce : ita non unquam similem experiare dolorem
    et faveant votis numina cuncta tuis.
quodque mihi eripuit mors inmatura iuventae,
    id tibi victuro proroget ulterius.' [82]

Even from the few inscriptions read, it is clear, as
Galletier says, that in spite of all their exaggerations
and conventionalities these epitaphs express a traditional
ideal on which society sought to model reality.   He con-
tinues in a significant paragraph :

"Grâce aux poèmes funéraires nous pouvons nous faire une
idée plus exacte de la matrone romaine et son rôle dans la famille.
Nous ne la voyons pas sous son vrai jour dans les textes littéraires,
si l'on en excepte quelques lettres de Cicéron et de Pline.   Son
image est déformée et ridicule dans le théâtre de Plaute ; les
héroïnes des poètes élégiaques appartiennent à la classe très
spéciale du demi-monde romain ; les historiens ne s'attachent
guère qu'aux figures surhumaines ou aux âmes criminelles.   Sur
les tombes, grandes dames et riches matrones coudoient les femmes
qui veillèrent au foyer des petites gens, des affranchis ou des
esclaves." [83]

---

[82] B. 995.   [83] Galletier, *op. cit.*, p. 122.

The portrayal of devotion between these men and women of the middle and lower classes shows great contrasts according to period or temperament. I have selected four which may represent Republican simplicity and reserve, flowering of emotion in fine literary form, torrent of unrestrained feeling, and Christian fervor and faith expressed in a cento of imitations.

The Republican epitaph is that of Aurelia Philematium [84] already referred to as one that in form approached the dialogue since wife and husband both speak, although neither addresses the other directly. The husband Aurelius was a freedman and a butcher. He praised his wife's chastity, her fidelity, her frugality and her devotion to duty. Philematium's angular figure stands out as stiff and clear as her own words and her husband's. Their reserved feeling finds expression in only eleven lines.

The next inscription is a joint epitaph for husband and wife.[85] Its theme is the quotation from Vergil in line 25, *fortunati ambo*,[86] for its serene and beautiful verses celebrate the long felicity on earth of Rhodanthion and his faithful Victoria, her devotion to his memory after his death, their reunion in the grave. Rhodanthion was full of years when he died, but he was blessed in life and happy in death ; no wonder, for his life had been roses, roses all the way, as though his name had been its keynote. After his wife had closed his eyes in death, she lived sick with the pain of her loss, but since she could not oppose fate, she did all she could : she kept true to him even unto death.

Fortunate both, for if in death any glory remaineth,
  This is theirs : in one tomb lie those who lay in one bed.

[84] B. 959.   [85] B. 1142.   [86] *Aen.* IX. 446.

Fortunati ambo — siqua est, ea gloria mortis —
quos iungit tumulus, iunxerat ut thalamus.

Only the Latin of the whole inscription can convey
the Roman dignity and loyalty in this picture of married
life.

The next epitaph is still longer (fifty-two lines).[87]   It
comes from the end of the third or the beginning of the
fourth century.   It is the epitaph of Allia Potestas, a
freedwoman, and was composed by her patron who was
one of her lovers.   The meter is an irregular combination of hexameters and pentameters.   The unique character of the epitaph consists in its attempt to give a detailed and unveiled portrait of the woman whose charms
are celebrated : her beautiful eyes, golden hair, gleaming ivory face, small white breasts, shining legs..   Only
her hands were hard because she loved to work and
would do everything for herself.   She was the first up
in the morning, the last to go to bed at night.   But she
had the charm of Helen of Troy for her two lovers : one
house held three, one love bound three, while she lived.
She made her lovers friends, Orestes and Pylades to each
other, and kept them young.   Now she is dead and they
have parted and grow old.   An incredible menage, but
recorded with verisimilitude.   Another epitaph parallels
the situation for in it a certain Lesbia names with pride
her two lovers.[88]   It seems incongruous that the old Republican virtues should be heaped upon this Allia, yet
she is lauded not only as entrancing, but as strong, holy,
innocent, faithful, neat, sparing of words, obsequious
and industrious, with her work always in her hands.
Strange combination of Helen and Claudia !

The Christian inscription which I have selected as an

[87] Galletier, *op. cit.*, pp. 104–5, 167–68, 335–36.
[88] B. 973.   Cf. Plautus, *Stichus*, 729–33.

illustration of another period and sentiment is the epitaph of Nymfius, written by his wife Serena, probably in the fifth century.[89] It was found in Novempopulania and is now in the Museum of Tolosa. It consists of twenty-four lines and is written in elegiac couplets. It is a clear expression of devotion and Christian faith expressed in a cento made up of quotations from Latin poets of all periods.

In pattern, it falls into three different parts. First (1–4) the death of Nymfius is stated in the language of the church :

> Here he is buried, but there heaven his soul now enjoys.

> hic situs est, caelo mens pia perfruitur.

The second part (5–18) is a genuine laudation of a statesman in public life working for the good of the province. All Aquitania loved him as a father. The people applauded his entrance in the theater because of his beneficence. In the name of his country he summoned the council of elders and was the mouthpiece of his country to them. Senators and people are now mourning for him.

In the third part (19–24) his wife Serena expresses her own personal grief. She ends :

> Life was sweet with you and now your anxious companion
> Hopes for eternal life, hopes that this life will be brief.

> dulcis vita fuit tecum, comes anxia lucem
> aeternam sperans hanc cupit esse brevem.

The poem is clear, dignified, sorrowful. Its expression has a fine literary aura from beautiful words and careful contrasts. It is a surprise to find that such poetry

[89] B. 2099.

has been achieved by patchwork, and that the twenty-four
lines contain quotations and reminiscences of Catullus,
Lucretius, Vergil (5), Ovid, Petronius, Martial, Lucan,
Claudian.[90]

I have tried to compose from the sepulchral inscriptions a picture of the Roman woman : the few episodes
of her life that are mentioned, the ideal of her that
developed at different periods and the various forms of
expression which it assumed. The portrait would not
be complete without a sketch of the Child in the House :
there are so many epitaphs for children.

Birth and death are the two haunting facts in their
little lives. Three epitaphs give the cause of death. A
tile from a roof fell on little Proculus.[91] While little
Volusius was at play, two fierce bulls ran away from their
driver and crushed him.[92] A third boy declares that the
cruel hand of a witch snatched him from his parents.[93]

The epitaphs of children are for the most part very
short, one or two couplets. A child speaks for himself
a lament over the brevity of his life. A mother sorrows
over her dead baby, or, dying herself, mourns for her deserted children. A recurring thought is that the parents
perform for the child rites which he should have carried
out for them.[94] Tenderness and pathos color the small
poems.

Born was I only for tears, a babe who to all was a sorrow.
Here now buried I lie, little my worth to my own.

[90] 1. Lucret. IV. 453, Cat. 64, 122, Verg. *Aen.* VIII. 406.
    3. Verg. *Aen.* II. 253.
    10. Ovid, *Met.* VII. 450, Claudian VIII. 259.
    12. Verg. *Georg.* II. 509, Lucan VII. 12.
    14. Mart. VIII. 1–2.
    16. Lucan, III. 104.
    19. Verg. *Aen.* XI. 62, Auson. *parent.* 16, 10, Claudian, *carm. min.* 30, 105.
    21. Verg. *Aen.* VI. 528, Petronius, 124, 267.
[91] B. 1060.   [92] B. 1059.   [93]. B. 987.   [94] B. 1486, 1168, 1156, 1479.

First was this year of my life ; I had hardly entered my second,
　When from its opening door Proserpine snatched me away.

Nata set in lachrimas solum, dolor omnibus in[fans
　hic sita sum, vixi tempus inane me[is.
annus erat vitae primus, mox deinde secundi
　liminibus rapuit me sibi Persephone.[95]

In another, a son laments his mother who after her
husband died had been to him both mother and father.[96]
Again a father laments the loss of wife and daughter in
one day.[97]　A young mother dead in childbirth says she
gave her life for her son, but does not know who will
care for her baby.[98]　Another mother prays that her
daughter may pattern her life after her own.

This is my prayer for my child that all of her days she remain pure,
　That from my life she may learn only her husband to love.

Opto meae caste contingat vivere natae,
　ut nostro exemplo discat amare virum.[99]

Fuscinilla laments that at twenty-three she was snatched
away from her three children and her husband, whom
she loved.[100]　Many epitaphs like these full of real feeling show the affection of the Romans for their children,
that same tenderness which in literature found expression in Catullus' wedding hymn with its picture of little
Torquatus and in Martial's epigrams for small Erotion.

It is natural to ask after reading these epitaphs of husbands, wives and children, and feeling the genuine sorrow in them, whether those who suffered worked out any
philosophy to solve the meaning of life and death.　The
inscriptions of the Republic, most of them formal, official
and aristocratic, do not contain individual reflections on
life, for man is viewed in relation to the state.　And even
regret over premature death comes from the fact that

[95] B. 1161.　　　　　[96] B. 2103.　　　　　[97] B. 1281.
[98] B. 2115.　　　　　[99] B. 1287.　　　　　[100] B. 1306.

the young man has not been able by his own exploits to equal the glory of his ancestors. Galletier in his summary of the philosophy of the dead points out that in the early Empire three moods appear in the inscriptions : pessimism arising either from the hardness of life or from the separation from dear ones caused by death : a cynical Epicureanism which finds the only reality in material and terrestrial joys ; and midway between these two extremes a fortitude which sees death as the inevitable blow of fate and tries to accept it with becoming strength and courage.[101]   To these attitudes should of course be added a fourth, the Christian faith which hopes for a blessed immortality.   These points of view, which recur in different periods and different parts of the Empire, are more a matter of temperament than of time. One man makes such moan as this :

Short life is better by far for mortals than many long years are,
   Since for a little time soul of man is in bloom.
But with old age comes grief and length of days renews sorrows.

Vita brevis longo melior mortalibus aevo,
   nam parvo spatio floruit haec anima. . .
de senio luctus, senium fletu renovatur.[102]

Then a jovial good-liver speaks.

Here I am in my tomb.   Primus my name.   I was famous.
Lived I on Lucrine oysters.   Falernian wine I drank often.
Bathing and drinking and loving were what helped pass my long
   lifetime.

Hoc ego su in tumulo Primus notissimus ille.
vixi Lucrinis, potabi saepe Falernum,
balnia vina Venus mecum senuere per annos.[103]

A more spiritual exclamation comes from a father.

101 Galletier, *op. cit.*, pp. 71–92.
102 B. 1203, 1–2, 7.   103 B. 1318, 1–3.

Honored was my old age and now in the fullness of long days
  Called to the gods am I.   Children, pray why do you mourn ?

Functus honorato senio plenusque dierum
  evocor ad superos : pignora, quid gemitis ? [104]

The Christian epitaphs often show exultation when
the earthly tabernacle is dissolved over a building not
made with hands.

Well this mean tomb will hold my body and give me sepúlture.
  This shall be the house which to my Manes belongs.
But how well my soul in beauty soars upward to heaven !
  One eternal day sheds on the future its light.

Tam bene reliquias n(ostras) hoc vi[le sepulcrum
  condet et haec] n(ostris) Manibus aedis erit,
quam ben [e caelum animus petit et pul] cherrimus ille
  clarificat Man [es perpetuusque dies.[105]

Few of the dead give advice and what is given is simple.
There are ancient versions of

> Eat, drink and be merry, for tomorrow we die,

and

> Say not the struggle nought availeth.

A simple Epicurean invitation is often issued from the
tomb :

> Eat, drink, play, come.

> es bibe lude veni.[106]

Young girls are urged to gather roses while they may.

Play and be happy, O maidens, while life will suffer your pastime.
  Often a sudden fate carries young beauties away.

ludite felices, patitur dum vita, puellae :
  saepe et formosas fata sinistra ferunt.[107]

[104] B. 1277.   [105] B. 2078.   [106] B. 1500.   [107] B. 1167, 5–6.

Again virtue is urged on men as its own reward.

Father was I to sons.   I saw my sons and dear grandsons.
Brave was my life and my deeds have made my years famous
always.
No foul tongue attacks aught that my years have achieved.
Learn, O mortals, to pass through life beyond taint of suspicion.
So one who lives without sin wins at the end his discharge.

et genui et vidi iuvenes carosq. nepotes.
vitae pro meritis claros transegimus annos,
quos nullo lingua crimine laedit atrox.
discite mortales sine crimine degere vitam :
sic meruit, vixit qui sine fraude, mori.[108]

This same nobility colors the whole epitaph of Macrobius of Parma.

I who endured much travel and suffered various labors
That with justice to all wealth of my own I might gain,
Now on dying relinquish whatever my hands have acquired.
This one house alone can to my Manes belong.
Near me lies my wife attesting our merited honors ;
Two whom life had joined, now not divided by death.
Sweet was life while it lasted for us.   Our ages were equal.
One love bound us both.   Now we are held in one peace.
Learn, O ye who read, to extend your fame by your merits.
These my verses prove there are rewards for the good.

Ille ego, qui varios cursus variumq. labor(em)
sustinui ut iustas conciliaret opes,
transmisi moriens rerum quaecunque paravi,
haec tamen ad Manes pertinet una domus.
et iuxta coniunx meritos testatur honores
aeternum retinens consociata torum.
nos aetate pares dulcis, dum vita manebat,
unus amor iunxit, nunc premit una quies.
discite qui legitis, factis extendere famam :
ut probat hic titulus, non perit esse bonos.[109]

I have tried in this essay to let the Latin elegiac inscriptions tell their own stories.   If from house-walls of

[108] B. 1238, 24-28.   [109] B. 1273.

Pompeii, marble tombstones along the Appian Way, rock-cut tomb of Sardinia, and many a monument in northern Africa the common people of ancient Italy have spoken to you I am pleased.   I shall be satisfied only if I have made these little poems, with all their crudities, banalities, repetitions and imitations, seem the expression of genuine feeling, not without beauty, and a priceless source of first-hand information for the private life of men and women whom formal literature neglected.

Death could capture their lives, but still after death their fame
    waxes.
Perished their bodies, but ever upon men's lips live their names.

tollere mors vitam potuit, post fata superstes
fama viget.   periit corpus, sed nomen in ore est.[110]

I hope that I may have persuaded some of you to accept the invitation which still cries out from many a sculptured slab.

Stranger if you are not weary, if this appeal is not a burden,
    Read my name, I beg.   Read the few words on my tomb.
Child was I of freedmen, of parents poor, yet both noble.
    Through my mother's care, taught was I many an art.
Husband had I of the same age young and noble and gracious.
    Dead I lie here now.   Sacred this little abode.
Now that you have read, O weary traveler, pass on.
    Sweet be the light to you.   Light be the earth upon me.

Hospes, si non es[t] lasso tibi forte molestum,
    oramus lecto nomine pauca legas.
sum libertinis ego nata parentibus ambis
    pauperibus censu, moribu[s] ingenuis.
sed m[atr]onali nutrita [pe]r omnia cura
    artibus et cun]ctis sum decora[ta b]onis.
co. . . vitae . . . aeus iuvei . . . iainosus,
    h]ic defuncta piis sedib(us) ecce moror.
tu qui preteriens [legis]ti, lasse viator,
    sit tibi lux dulcis et mihi terra levis.[111]

III

SATIRE AND THE LATIN NOVEL

THE *Satyricon,* the earlier of the two extant Latin novels, is rooted deep in a philosophical school and draws from that source life for the shape of its branching tree. The *Satyricon* in form is a Menippean satire and in spirit is akin to the laughing Cynicism by which Menippus exposed the foibles and superstitions of mankind. Unfortunately little remains of this philosopher of Gadara who in the third century before Christ wrote Cynic dialogues and diatribes. To trace his influence in Latin satire and novel we must, by admitted anachronism, go to a Greek of the first and second century, and let Lucian reconstruct for us a picture of the Cynic and his teachings.[1] For the form of Menippus' satires, we can learn more from his Latin imitators, Varro, Seneca, Petronius.[2]

The Cynic philosopher is one of the legitimate, spiritual sons of Socrates, whose lineal descendants included by strange aberrations of mental heredity the Cynic preacher, who begat the Stoic, the Cyrenaic Hedonist who begat the Epicurean and the mystic Plato, father of all idealists. The most popular among all these later schools which tried to systematize the undogmatic teach-

[1] See R. Helm, *Lucian and Menipp,* Leipzig, 1906.
[2] See N. Terzaghi, *Per la Storia della Satira,* Torino, 1932.

ings of the great teacher was the Cynic philosophy. Or rather let us say the Cynic preaching. Stoicism, the child of the Cynic, was to develop into a formal and reasoned philosophy for the intelligentsia with a systematized cosmology, a physics and an ethics, but Cynicism remained a teaching of a way of life, brought down from the skies to earth. So the Cynic teacher, Antisthenes, Diogenes, Crates, in symbolic garb of cloak, wallet and staff, talked on street corners and in open squares to the plain man of the streets. And these Hyde Park orators of the Greek world assailed with unhampered liberty of speech the conventions and superstitions of society, hoping by their genial raillery to free the spirit of the humble and the downtrodden, to give him self-reliance, a new sense of permanent values and an inner peace. For the burden of the Cynic's teaching was that one who renounces all, gains all, and the essential is already in the possession of each human being. These Cynic sermons were informal talks, which used the Socratic method of interrogation and dialogue ; only, as the preacher answered his own questions, setting up a fictitious interlocutor whom he could oppose and convince, the form of such colloquy came to be called a diatribe. It was a kind of monologue-dialogue that was very effective for informal presentation of ethical teaching, as Horace has shown in his later use of it.

Now it is Lucian who paints more vividly than any other writer the Cynic as the satirist of mankind, so from his dialogues written in the second century we will try to recreate a picture of Menippus and his kind. Lucian's life was as variegated as his writing. This Syrian, born in Commagene, lived in Ionia, Greece, Italy, Gaul, Antioch and Athens. His long life extended through the rule of Antoninus Pius, Marcus Aurelius,

Lucius Verus, Commodus and perhaps Pertinax. A rhetorician and a satirist he yet held under Commodus a well-paid government position in Egypt. He wrote in Greek. And as he seemed to belong to no one country, so he could be claimed by no one philosophical school. He was interested in all life and all philosophy and his literary object seems to have been to amuse by a genial satire of human life. Temperamentally he seems closely related to the Cynic whom he describes.

In the Dialogue called "Philosophies for Sale," the auctioneer, Hermes, lets the Cynic advertise his own wares to a possible purchaser. This Cynic declares that he is a citizen of the world, a man who patterns his life after Hercules in making war on pleasures and aiming to purify life ; "a liberator of men and a physician to their ills . . . an interpreter of truth and free speech." Then he informs the buyer of the course of training he would lay down for him.

"First, after taking you in charge, stripping you of your luxury and shackling you to want, I will put a short cloak on you. Next I will compel you to undergo pain and hardships, sleeping on the ground, drinking nothing but water and filling yourself with any food that comes your way. As for your money, in case you have any, if you follow my advice you will throw it into the sea forthwith. You will take no thought for marriage or children or native land : all that will be sheer nonsense to you, and you will leave the house of your fathers and make your home in a tomb or a deserted tower or even a jar. Your wallet will be full of lupines, and of papyrus rolls written on both sides. Leading this life you will say that you are happier than the Great King ; and if anyone flogs you or twists you on the rack, you will think that there is nothing painful in it." [3]

When the Cynic goes on to urge that his pupil's conduct must be bold, his language barbarous, his expres-

[3] In *Lucian* with an English translation by A. M. Harmon, in *The Loeb Classical Library*, New York, 1915, II. p. 467.

sion, walk and bearing savage and wild, his life solitary, his habits uncivilized, the buyer refuses to purchase a way of life so ugly and inhuman.

In another dialogue, "Zeus Catechized," the Cynic confounds the King of the Gods as in "Philosophies for Sale" he did the plain man. For he proves that the power of fate is supreme even over the gods, that through fortune's changes the good suffer and the wicked flourish, and that the prayers of men to the gods are of no avail in affecting their destiny. In "Charon," the futility of all objects of prayer, wealth, rank, houses, lands, is demonstrated since all skeletons look alike after death and an added corollary is that sepulture is therefore useless.

In the "Dialogues of the Dead" Diogenes invites Menippus to come down to Hades to find rich material for his laughter. And Menippus is rewarded for his descent by seeing that heroes, kings, philosophers, millionaires, prophets, beauties are mere bones now, stripped skulls, eyeless sockets,

"Imperial Caesar, dead and turned to clay."

As in these little "Dialogues of the Dead" and in the longer dialogue, "The Downward Journey," the Cynic descends into Hades, so in "Icaromenippus," the Cynic, Menippus himself here, ascends into heaven to see from that lofty viewpoint of the gods the earth in true perspective and the meaning of men's institutions and philosophies. In that aviator's vista he sees cities of men like busy ant-hills, each individual an infinitesimal atom, all men's efforts futile. And this discouraging vision of man's littleness is confirmed by Zeus' description of their philosophies, for he tells the gods in council that the little schools of these tiny creatures, Stoic, Academy,

Epicurean, Peripatetic, are all merely like the masks and gorgeous robes of actors and when they are removed nothing is left but the ridiculous little manikin hired to play his part for seven drachmas. So histrionic, so meretricious are all the poses of the philosophers. Menippus after sending his soul to the invisible in journeys downward and upward learns at last only that he himself is heaven and hell.

The strange part of this Cynic creed is its attraction through centuries for many men. Yet a gospel that proclaimed to the poor that they could possess wealth of spirit, that offered to all the greatest blessings of the world, "Wisdom, Self-Sufficiency, Truth, Frankness, Freedom," can find in all ages its followers. As Livingstone says, "The Cynics are the spiritual kinsmen of the Indian Fakir, of the anchorite of the desert, of the begging friar : of Rousseau in the solitudes of the Hermitage, of Thoreau in the woods of Walden ; there is something of them in the muscular Christian and in the bearer of the white man's burden : and something in all caravaners and campers-out." [4]

From Cicero and Quintilian in their comments on the type of satire which Varro wrote we learn something of the form of Menippus, for Varro is said to have mingled prose and verse [5] and to have imitated Menippus in the raillery with which he presented his ethical themes.[6] Terzaghi in his careful study of the history of satire [7] comes to the conclusion that the development of the Menippean form was something like this. Bion, the Borysthenite,[8] wrote in prose, but added quotations of

---

[4] R. W. Livingstone, *The Mission of Greece*, Oxford, 1928, p. 37.
[5] Quintilian, X. 1, 95. See also, Probus on Verg. *Ec.* VI, 31, and Macrobius, *Sat.* I. 11, 42.
[6] Cic., *Acad. Post.* I. ii, 8.   [7] Terzaghi, *op. cit.*, pp. 42-51.
[8] See Horace, Epistles, II. 2, 60.

poetry, either in their original form or adapted. Menippus wrote in prose and verse, using generally quotations of poetry but sometimes introducing poetic passages of his own. Varro wrote in prose and in poetry which was always original. Then the development of satire divided into two parts : one a line of satire entirely in poetry, Lucilius, Horace, Persius and Juvenal ; the other the Menippean in prose and original poetry, Seneca and Petronius.

Terzaghi thinks that the originality of Varro consisted in composing virtually all the poetry in his satires while Menippus quoted most of his poetical passages. Lucian who wished to revive Menippus and took him as a model used many quotations and parodies of poets. Terzaghi goes on to say that we know little about the themes of Menippus, but we know that he satirized the vices and foibles of men from the Cynic viewpoint and with the Cynic tolerance.

Certainly we can follow Terzaghi in his tracing of the two lines of development of the form of Latin satire : the Menippean mixture of prose and poetry, the all-verse satire. To understand what satire went into the *Satyricon* of Petronius and the *Metamorphoses* of Apuleius we need to study the form of Menippean satire and the *Satyricon ;* the satirical treatment of a special subject, a banquet, used by virtually all the satirists and in the *Satyricon ;* and the point of view of the Cynic preaching which appears in both Roman satire and novels.

M. Terentius Varro of Reate (116–27 B.C.) was a Sabine by birth and character. Austere virtue and indefatigable labor characterized his life and ideals. Although he was a scholar of encyclopaedic learning, he was a man of affairs who served the state in peace as tribune and aedile, in war as lieutenant under Pompey when he cleared the sea of pirates and again in Spain in the Civil War. Later he became reconciled to Julius Caesar and in recognition of amity he was appointed librarian of the public library which Caesar planned. Because of this friendship he narrowly escaped being proscribed by Antony ; indeed, his villa and private library were seized, but he lived on devoting himself to learning. He is said to have written four hundred and ninety books or more on an incredible range of subjects, including history, biography, antiquities, linguistics, philosophy and education.[9] But here we are concerned only with his *Saturae Menippeae*. Their one hundred and fifty books exist unfortunately only in brief and scattered fragments, but these are enough to permit reconstruction of his themes and his point of view.

Mommsen has well characterized him as "a man full of old Roman indignation at the pitiful times and full of old Roman humour."[10] And perhaps Varro's own character appears in his *Sexagessis,* the Rip Van Winkle who having gone to sleep at the age of ten awakes after fifty years to find nothing left of the Rome which he had known. In place of the ancient virtues, treachery, shamelessness, impiety reign. There is never an Aeneas to carry his father off — except by poison ! No one obeys the laws : "give and take" is the motto of all. And there is no use in the state for the old : throw them off the bridge into the Tiber !

It is from this point of view of pristine righteousness that Varro criticizes his world. Philosophers, women, gourmands, drunkards are all butts of his satire. The quaint titles with their mixture of Greek and Latin are

⁹ See J. Wight Duff, *A Literary History of Rome from the Origins to the Close of the Golden Age,* New York, 1927, pp. 330–38.
¹⁰ T. Mommsen, *The History of Rome,* translated by W. P. Dickson, New York, 1887, IV. p. 706,

illuminating for his themes : *Est Modus Matulae*, περὶ μέθης, "A Wine Jar Has its Limit, On Drunkenness," *Aborigines*, περὶ ἀνθρώπων φύσεως, "The Primitives, On the Nature of Man," *Papia papae*, περὶ ἐγκωμίων, "Fie ! Fie ! On Flatteries." Several titles show that the Cynics' "Dog-World" was featured. And through various fragments runs laughter at the quiddities and the quoddities of Sceptics and Stoics until finally Varro declares :

> No sick man ever dreamed a thing so strange
> Which some philosopher does not call true.
>
> postremo, nemo aegrotus quicquam somniat
> tam infandum, quod non aliquis dicat philosophus.[11]

Over and over the avaricious man is stigmatized. Mad indeed is the avaricious, for if he should be given into custody to any land in the world, still driven on by the same disease of thieving, he would seek something from himself and get together something for a slave's hoard.[12] Yet the heart is not freed by golden treasures ; the mountains of the Persians, the halls of rich Crassus do not take from men's souls cares and fears.[13]

Women now share the extravagance of men. Of old reverence and chastity reigned in the home. The lady of the house spun her wool and at the same time kept her eye on the pot on the fire to keep the dinner from burning.[14] But now the girl begs her father for a pound of eye-beads, the wife begs her husband for a peck of pearls.[15] The Lady's eyelashes are darkened. The dimple in her chin indented by the finger of Love shows her softness. Her long neck white as marble is set off by the royal purple of her tunic. Six little curls stray

---

11 F. Buecheler, *Petronii Saturae et Liber Priapeorum ; Varronis et Senecae Saturae Similesque Reliquiae*, Berlin, 1904, *Eumenides*, VI. (122.)
12 Buecheler, *op. cit.*, *Eumenides*, X. (126.)
13 Buecheler, *op. cit.*, 'Ανθρωπόπολις, I. (36.)
14 Buecheler, *op. cit.*, Γεροντοδιδάσκολος, I. (181) and X. (190.)
15 Buecheler, *op. cit.*, *Marcipor*, XV. (283.)

down her neck.   Her shining eyes display the merriment
of her soul.   Her little rosy mouth is parted in unrestrained laughter.[16]   Formerly once or twice a year a
wife was given a ride in her husband's carriage.   Now
all rush to Rome.   Of old the bridegroom timidly approached his bride.   Now wife says to husband : "Do
you not know what Ennius wrote,

> 'Three times in war I'd risk my life
> To once in childbirth ?' " [17]

Varro's ideal for simple family life, set forth in *Manius,*
"The Early Riser," has been delightfully reconstructed
by Mommsen :

"Manius summons his people to rise with the sun, and in person
conducts them to the scene of their labours.   The youths make
their own bed, which labour renders soft to them, and supply
themselves with waterpot and lamp.   Their drink is the clear
fresh spring, their fare bread, and onions as a relish.   Everything
prospers in house and field.   The house is no work of art ; but
an architect might learn symmetry from it.   Care is taken of the
field, that it shall not be left disorderly or waste, or go to ruin
through slovenliness and neglect ; in return the grateful Ceres
wards off damage from the produce, that the high-piled sheaves
may gladden the heart of the husbandman.   Here hospitality still
holds good ; everyone who has but imbibed mother's milk is welcome.   The bread-pantry and wine-vat and the store of sausages
on the rafters, lock, and key are at the service of the traveller, and
piles of food are set before him ; contented sits the sated guest,
looking neither before nor behind, dozing by the hearth in the
kitchen.   The warmest double-wool sheep-skin is spread as a
couch for him.   Here people still as good burgesses obey the
righteous law, which neither out of envy injures the innocent,
nor out of favour pardons the guilty.   Here they speak no evil
against their neighbours.   Here they trespass not with their feet
on the sacred hearth, but honour the gods with devotion and with
sacrifices, throw to the familiar spirit his little bit of flesh into his
appointed little dish, and when the master of the household dies,

---

[16] Buecheler, *op. cit., Papia Papae,* I. (370.), II. (371.), III. (372.), VI. (375.)
[17] Buecheler, *op. cit.,* Γεροντοδιδάσκολος, VIII. (188.), VII. (187.), IX. (189.)

accompany the bier with the same prayer with which those of his
father and of his grandfather were borne forth." [18]

Enough has been quoted to show the spirit and the
themes of Varro's Menippean satires. Duff summarizes
well both their content and form.

"Even in their fragmentary state, one can detect the astounding
variety of range on social, ethical, and literary topics. Varro
sketches life around him without invective. It is the old racy
satura revived, with a strong dash of cynicism imported from the
Greek. Plebeian expressions jostle learned terms. Dramatic situations and offhand dialogue form the framework to point a
moral. The ancient mythology, and 'the dog-world of Diogenes'
are laid under contribution now for serious and now for comic
effect. Two threads of thought run on continuously — one, the
absurdity of much Greek philosophizing, with which Varro would
contrast his own homely lessons ; the other, the tightening grip of
luxury, with which Varro would contrast the good old days." [19]

The one ancient Menippean satire extant in nearly
complete form is the *Apocolocyntosis,* or *Ludus de morte
Claudii,* "The Pumpkinification of Claudius," by Seneca.
Varro's work is in fragments. Petronius' *Satyricon* is
also fragmentary and is more of a novel than a Menippean satire. Hence the *Apocolocyntosis* is of the greatest interest for our subject.

L. Annaeus Seneca (4 B.C.–65 A.D.), second son of the
so-called "rhetor," born in Spain, was one of those provincial Romans of the early Empire who came to great
power in the Capital. His career was as full of vicissi-
tudes as his character was of inconsistencies. As quaes-
tor, he was threatened with death by Caligula. As philosopher, he was exiled to Corsica for alleged intrigues
with princesses. Recalled in 49, as praetor he was tutor
to the young Nero and directed the five good years of his

[18] Mommsen, *op. cit.,* vol. IV. p. 713 ; Buecheler, *op. cit., Manius,* I–XXII.
(247–68.)
[19] J. Wight Duff, *op. cit.,* p. 335.

ward's reign.   As a millionaire minister he aroused the
envy of his master and was forced to a Stoic's death by his
own hand.   His philosophical interests, his melodramatic adaptations, and his satirical observation of life
found expression in works as widely different as *Dialogues* and *Moral Epistles, Tragedies* and the satire on
Claudius.[20]

It is the form and the spirit of the *Apocolocyntosis*
which we are to study, not the many controversies which
have arisen over it.   These have to do with the double
title, the doubtful authorship, the political propaganda
for Nero contained in it, the significance of the whole
satire for the attitude of the Romans toward the divinity
of the Roman Emperor and indeed their belief in the
gods.   The problems and reasonable solutions of them
have been neatly summarized by Allan P. Ball in the
introduction to his edition of *The Satire of Seneca on the
Apotheosis of Claudius.*[21]

The double name inferred from Dio Cassius [22] is reminiscent of Varro's mixed titles in Greek and Latin.   The
title *Apocolocyntosis* perhaps was suggestive or symbolic
for the deification of a dunderhead, as there is no reference to pumpkinification in the satire in its present form.
The chief arguments against Seneca's authorship of the
satire are the contrast between its attack and the laudation of Claudius by Seneca in the *Consolatio ad Poly-
bium,* the meanness of its personalities, the silence of all
Latin authors about the existence of such a work by
Seneca.   But the inconsistencies in Seneca's life and character are enough to account for the first two points, and

[20] On Seneca the Philosopher, see J. Wight Duff, *A Literary History of
Rome in the Silver Age from Tiberius to Hadrian,* New York, 1927, pp. 196–
278.
[21] My introductory material is drawn largely from this work.
[22] Dio Cassius, LXI. 35.

the third point may be answered by the fact that only a small portion of Latin literature is extant so that such silence is not conclusive.

Points in favor of Seneca's authorship are his resentment against Claudius for causing his banishment and his desire to secure return from exile in Corsica by Nero's favor. Moreover, the irony with which both Emperor and Gods are treated is consistent with the brilliant wit of Seneca, the Moralist. The best working hypothesis for a study of the satire seems to be that it was written by Seneca the Philosopher. However, the question of authorship hardly affects its literary form.

The *Apocolocyntosis* is written in a mixture of prose and poetry and the poetry is both quoted and original. Of the quotations only four are assigned to authors: Homer, Varro, Messala Corvinus, and Horace ; [23] but reminiscences of Euripides and Vergil among others are recognizable. Original poems use hexameters, anapaests, iambic senarii. Part of the irony of the whole work is this very use of poetry. Hercules and Claudius greet each other with lines from Homer. Hercules later "declaims like a tragedian in iambic trimeter" and "at the end of the story Claudius' futile efforts with the broken dice-box are described in hexameters for which the only excuse seems to be their heroic inappropriateness." [24]

Not only in such mixture of prose and poetry, but also in language does Seneca seem to be following Varro, for the diction mingles the mock-heroic style with the colloquial use of proverbs, of popular jokes and puns, of plebeian words, diminutives, and grammar. Varro too once wrote a political satire, the Τρικάρανος, on the first

---

[23] *Apoc.* 5, 8, 10, 13.
[24] A. P. Ball, *The Satire of Seneca on the Apotheosis of Claudius,* New York, 1902. p. 63.

Triumvirate so he may have been the model for Seneca's theme as well as for his style.

The temper of the times toward the Emperor Claudius after his death may be seen from the fact that when Nero who delivered his funeral oration, praised his wisdom and foresight, no one present restrained his laughter.   And this too, Tacitus adds, although the speech was composed by Seneca in his usual elegant and pleasing style.[25]   A court which could be derisive during the emperor's funeral ceremonies would easily have tolerated and relished the witty skit on Claudius' deification.

No paraphrase can give an adequate impression of the rapidity and wit, the cruelty and the irreverence of this mordaunt satire.   The *Apocolocyntosis* begins like history with the date, but variations are rung on it in both prose and poetry, and as for evidence for it, who ever demanded from historians sworn witnesses ?   Here is the fact : Claudius began to die, but could not end.   So Mercury who had always been delighted by his genius appealed to the fates to let him off with the remarkable argument that here is a man who cannot die although no one knew he had ever been born !

Clotho protested that she had wished to give him a bit more time so he could make the few foreigners who were left in the world (Greeks, Gauls, Spaniards, Britons), Roman citizens, clad in the toga, but she will indulge Mercury's desire.   Then in a long epic passage in hexameters reminiscent of Catullus the fates are described spinning the thread of life off for the old fool of a Claudius and on for the new star of a Nero.   And Apollo eloquently begs long life for the one who is like himself in face, in beauty, in song and in voice, in other words, for the artist Nero !

So good-bye to Claudius !   At last he bubbled up his

[25] Tacitus, *Ann.* xiii, 3.

breath and on that ceased to seem to live. There was public joy on earth, and divine perplexity in heaven when Claudius went up. Jupiter was informed that a tall stranger had arrived, who seemed to be threatening something, for he shook his head constantly ; his right foot was halting ; his speech a mumble so you could not tell whether he was Greek or Roman or of some other tribe. Jupiter dispatched Hercules since he had traveled all over the world, to ascertain the stranger's nationality. The hero and the emperor exchanged a few lines of greeting from Homer, but when Claudius, just to cap a quotation, and indicate that he was Caesar, spouted :

> From Troy winds blew me to Ciconian shores,

the goddess Fever, his escort, gave the lie to such autobiography and stated the plain fact that he was born at Lyons and, as a Gaul should, recaptured Rome.

Claudius protested with an "Off with her head" as usual. But Hercules then took him in hand and told him to stop playing the fool since he had come to the place where mice gnaw iron and only truth goes. To impress the stranger, Hercules, though a little in terror at this new monster, spouted tragically fourteen iambic trimeters of intimidation. Claudius then realized that he was no longer at Rome and the cock of the manure heap, so he implored Hercules to aid him.

Evidently he was successful for after a lacuna in which Hercules must have been won over, the scene changed to an assembly of gods, who were debating Hercules' proposal to deify Claudius. While they were considering what sort of a god he could possibly be made, Jupiter brought up a technical point that while strangers were in the House, the senators could not debate, so Claudius was escorted out. Janus then made a speech on the maj-

esty of the gods and the horror of transforming everybody
into a deity so that glory is turned into farce.   In spite of
this eloquence, Diespiter brought in a grandiloquent
motion for deification :

> "Whereas the divine Claudius is a relative of the divine Augus-
> tus and the divine Augusta, his grandmother, whom he himself
> deified, and whereas he greatly surpasses all mortals in wisdom,
> and whereas there should be some member of the state who can
> accompany Romulus in devouring boiled turnips, be it resolved
> that the divine Claudius from this day be a god with all the
> rights and privileges of the same, and that this decree be recorded
> in the *Metamorphoses* of Ovid !"

When the lobbying of Hercules seemed likely to secure
an affirmative vote on the motion, Augustus made a formal
protest (perhaps a parody of the Emperor's style).   He
reminded the Senate that never before since he was dei-
fied, has he uttered a word ; he has always minded his own
business.   Now shame and grief have forced speech.
"Was it for this," he asked, "that I made peace on land and
sea, composed civil wars, founded the city by laws,
adorned it with buildings ?   This man, Senators, who
looks unable to brush off a fly killed men as easily as a dog
sits down.   Think of the list of his murders !   Where
did he find a precedent for putting men to death without
trial ?   Certainly not in heaven, for only once has such
an event happened under Jupiter when in anger at Vul-
can, the king of the gods hurled him from the sky !   Do
you wish to make this murderer a god ?   This stammer-
ing monstrosity a deity ?"

After this eloquent peroration Augustus proposed a
substitute motion that Claudius be banished immediately
to the lower world.   It was voted at once and Mercury
led the condemned emperor downward.   En route
Claudius happened to spy his own funeral so he knew that
he was dead.   For they were singing a great funeral dirge

in anapaests. The nenia ironically praised Claudius' keen wit, his swift feet, his conquest of Britain and of the sea, his speedy judgments, and a very good judge was he, who will soon take the place of Aeacus in the lower world.

Claudius was so delighted with these praises that he wanted to watch the spectacle longer, but Mercury hurried him on to Hades. There his freedman, Narcissus, met him and acted as herald of his arrival. Big, black Cerberus terrified the Emperor because he had only a little white female dog at home as a pet. When a great crowd of Roman officials, knights, and freedmen gathered about the newcomer, Claudius was delighted and exclaimed : "Why ! The place is full of my friends ! How did you get here ?" Pedo Pompeius rebuked his absentmindedness by retorting : "Do *you* ask that, you who sent us here, you who are the murderer of all your friends ?"

Claudius was then taken before the judgment seat of Aeacus ; the charges against him were read. Aeacus, à la the criminal, heard only one side of the case, and condemned the accused. His punishment was then decreed : that he should rattle dice in a box with holes in the bottom forever. The wretched Emperor's futile labor was described in seven epic hexameters. I quote Rouse's humorous translation :

"For when he rattled with the box, and thought he now had got 'em
The little cubes would vanish thro' the perforated bottom.
Then he would pick 'em up again, and once more set a' trying :
The dice but served him the same trick : away they went a-flying.
So still he tries, and still he fails ; still searching long he lingers ;
And every time the tricksy things go slipping thro' his fingers.
Just so when Sisyphus at last once gets there with his boulder,
He finds the labour all in vain — it rolls down off his shoulder." [26]

[26] In *Petronius* with an English translation by Michael Heseltine, *Seneca*

This was almost the merry end, but not quite, for Caligula turned up and claimed the man as his slave on the ground that Claudius was presented to Caligula, who gave him to Aeacus, who gave him to his freedman, Menander, to be his clerk at law. This was the end of the pumpkin-headed Emperor.

This running paraphrase of the *Apocolocyntosis* has perhaps demonstrated its kinship with the ironic cynicism of Menippus as revealed in Lucian. Its outspoken frankness, its biting wit, its brutal personalities, its ugly realism, its irreverence toward gods, heroes and rulers all contribute to its Cynic laughter. The unexpected turns, the mock-heroic verses increase the humor. And the rapidity of movement in the short piece accentuates the sharpness and the brilliancy of the satire.

The other Menippean satire extant, which is probably contemporary with the *Apocolocyntosis,* is the *Satyricon.* The title, which as it stands is a Greek genitive plural, appears also in the manuscripts as *Satirarum libri* or *Satyrici libri.* Probably *Satirae* evolved from *Satyrica* and the original title meant a romance dealing with things of a *satyr-like* character.[27]   Only parts of the fifteenth and sixteenth books exist, but they contain the priceless portion, "The Banquet of Trimalchio," which was found at Trau in Dalmatia only in the middle of the seventeenth century. The author is now generally admitted to be Petronius Arbiter and the time the reign of Nero. The nature of the work suits both this period and the character of Petronius as it is sketched by Tacitus.[28]

Petronius in an age when Stoic virtue was an offense

Apocolocyntosis with an English translation by W. H. D. Rouse. *The Loeb Classical Library,* New York, 1930, pp. 405-7.

[27] See B. E. Perry, "Petronius and the Comic Romance," *Class. Phil.* xx (1925), pp. 33-34.

[28] Tacitus, *Ann.* xvi, 18-19.

assumed the rôle of the Eiron or ironic fool which J. A. K. Thomson has described so subtly.[29]   Since the gods and the kings of earth are always jealous creatures, each an Alazon or pretentious Impostor, the Ironical Man will lie low, to escape their notice, will pretend to be of little importance in order to be free to pursue his own life in some security and happiness.   So Tacitus' Petronius made his way to fame by laziness, not by industry as others did.   His words and deeds were models of elegant simplicity.   As proconsul in Bithynia, as consul in Rome, he was energetic and efficient.   Out of office, he returned to his vices or to his imitation of vices and bore the title of *elegantiae arbiter* at Nero's court.

In spite of all this careful nonchalance and studied humility, the Eiron aroused the envy of Nero's favorite, Tigellinus, and suffered the condemnation of the Emperor.   Petronius then met death as ironically as he had lived.   For he did not hurry to his ordered suicide, but had his veins opened, then bound again.   He talked with his friends, not on serious matters or themes of fortitude. And he listened to his friends who did not talk on the immortality of the soul or the consolations of philosophy, but read him light and graceful poems.   He rewarded some of his slaves with gifts, punished others with flogging.   He went to dinner, he took a siesta, to make his execution resemble a natural death.   At the very end the Ironical Man threw off his mask and gave a sword-thrust. He did not flatter Nero or Tigellinus or any of those in power.   But he wrote down the enormities of the emperor and his novel debaucheries under the names of (his) mignons and mistresses and sent the account sealed to Nero.   The Eiron on dying defied and exposed the tyrant who had corrupted his life and conditioned his death.

[29] J. A. K. Thomson, *Irony*, London, 1926.

Such a character as Petronius is peculiarly fit for the author of the *Satyricon*. The book is a cross between a Menippean satire, composed in prose and verse, and a Milesian tale, an indecent story pointed usually by sex. It owes something to the mime, the epic and the Greek erotic romance. It may have had a Greek comic romance as its prototype.[30] In any case the whole is colored by the Cynic irony. Any analysis of the *Satyricon* will be imperfect because of its fragmentary condition, yet we must attempt a brief outline of the plan, the subject matter and the characters before studying the style and spirit. The *Satyricon* appears to be a novel of slight plot and innumerable episodes told in the first person as a narrative of adventure. Various theories have been advanced about its motivation : that it was a satire of Nero under the disguise of Trimalchio ; that it was a satire of the freedmen of the court, written to amuse Nero ; that Trimalchio represented not Nero, but Claudius ; that it was a prose epic with the theme, the wrath of the offended Priapus. But all such theories prove in application so inadequate that it seems better to assume that it was written as a piece of fiction to amuse the author and to give amusement to his readers.

The narrator is Encolpius, one of a pair of rascals who with his companion, Ascyltos, and a pet boy of theirs, called Giton, slip in and out of disreputable and scandalous escapades. Among the scenes of their adventures are the portico of a school of rhetoric, a brothel, a marketplace of peddlers, various bed rooms, the magnificent dining room of the millionaire Trimalchio, an inn, an art-gallery, the deck of a ship, the city of Croton, and a witch's work-shop, a kaleidoscopic background. Through

---

30 See B. E. Perry, "Petronius and the Comic Romance," *Class. Phil.* xx (1925), pp. 31–49.

these scenes the young men dash on their venal, amorous, rotten way. Part of the verve of their lives is their delight in observing the cities and the customs of men. Part of the excitement of the narrative is the rich coloring and the minute details with which the realistic picture is created. A great canvas of a world of vulgar, shrewd, common people is unrolled before us. Nothing is considered too indecent or unclean to have a place here. Yet the triumph of the art is the selection of the persons, the scenes, the details, the contrasts which make the whole such living realism.

Encolpius' straight narrative of the adventures of the vagabonds in the cities of southern Italy is diversified by stories within stories, for the freedman, Niceros, entertains at dinner with a tale of a werewolf ; Trimalchio caps his horrors with a story of a Cappadocian who turned blue and a changeling straw-boy ; and on shipboard Eumolpus to keep the peace relates the famous story of the Widow of Ephesus.[31]

The language of the novel is a veritable *farrago*, a hodge-podge of elegance and vulgarity, rhetoric and slang, the mock-heroic, the plebeian, the startlingly beautiful and the tritely proverbial. The diction is varied with the persons speaking and comments are dropped on the different ways of talking of the highbrow and the plain man as well as on different fashions in poetry.

The incidental verse adds immensely to the variety and spice of the narrative. By far the greater part of the poetry is written in hexameters. Elegiacs are the next favorite. Iambics and hendecasyllables are also used. The poems fall into a literary group, an ethical group, mock-heroics on unworthy subjects, love-poems. The literary group begins with a soaring passage in iambic

[31] *Sat.* 61–62, 63, 111–12.

trimeters by Agamemnon, a professor of rhetoric, on the glories of the old Roman education for oratory.[32] It includes a long poem of sixty-five iambics by Eumolpus on the fall of Troy, which was bound to suggest comparison with Vergil and perhaps for that reason brought a shower of stones on the offending poet's head at the end.[33] Another iambic poem of seventeen lines is attributed to Publilius Syrus and is quoted by Trimalchio to show the superiority of his style to Cicero's, a strange comparison ![34] The longest poem is an epic passage of two hundred and ninety-five hexameters on the Civil War clearly written as a parody of Lucan although that poet is never mentioned.[35] Disparaging comments on incidental poems are occasionally made : Trimalchio's epigram on Fortune's changes is said to be a monstrosity.[36] Eumolpus' attempts in both elegiacs and hendecasyllables at a dirge on the subject of hair are called the foolish trifles of a drunken bard.[37]

Poems on ethical subjects are introduced with irony to set off the character of the moralizer. Eumolpus, the professional poet, is always prosing poor lines on

"That which is hard to win is treasured most," [38]

or on the poverty of the virtuous orator, and the prosperity of the wicked, be he merchant, warrior, bootlicker or adulterer.[39] The worthless Ascyltos virtuously declaims elegiacs on the venality of the times, even in men who parade with the Cynic's wallet.[40] Trimalchio at the height of his prosperity scribbles down a few lines on the turns of Fortune's wheel.[41]

The same sort of irony is used in employing poetry for mock-heroic expression of unworthy subjects, some the

32 *Sat.* 5. 33 *Sat.* 89. 34 *Sat.* 55. 35 *Sat.* 119–24.
36 *Sat.* 55. 37 *Sat.* 109–10. 38 *Sat.* 93. 39 *Sat.* 83.
40 *Sat.* 14. 41 *Sat.* 55.

vilest.[42]   The corrupt Quartilla rants on the delights of
female conquest,[43] Tryphaena on the strength of a woman
scorned.[44]   Oenothea exalts her power as a witch in lofty
hexameters.[45]   Any vagabond may suddenly burst into
poetry :

> What a night that one was, O all ye gods !
>
> Qualis nox fuit illa, di deaeque.[46]

A deeper irony seems to infuse a set of really exquisite
lyrics written for a beauty named Circe whose character
clearly did not match her face, for her own maid described
her as one who hunted lovers among gladiators, slaves and
plebeians standing at the back of the theater.   Circe is
sung as the true Danaë.   A dainty picture of a bed of
flowers is painted for the scene of her embrace.   Desire
for her is compared to the elusive longing for a buried
treasure of gold hunted in a dream.[47]   Here the antithesis
is between the corrupt nature of the innamorata and the
pure beauty of the lyrics describing her.   Oftener, as we
have seen, the ironic contrast is between the supposed
character of the author of each poem and the nature of
the sentiments expressed in his poem.

This sophisticated raillery runs through the whole
novel and may be seen in the treatment of character, of
situation, of conversation, even of life itself.   Small vi-
gnettes of individuals are unforgettable.   Here are two
freedmen guests at Trimalchio's dinner.

"That man over there lying in the lowest place on the lowest couch
is worth 800,000 today.   He's come up from nothing.   Just lately
he was carrying loads of wood on his back.   But, as the saying
goes, he stole a fairy's cap and found some gold.   Well, I envy
nobody if a god gives him a gift.   You'd see he had just been a
slave, but he has a fine opinion of himself.   Lately he offered his
hut for rent with this sign : 'Caius Pompeius Diogenes will let

---

[42] *Sat.* 132.   [43] *Sat.* 18.   [44] *Sat.* 108.
[45] *Sat.* 134.   [46] *Sat.* 79.   [47] *Sat.* 126–28.

this apartment after July first ; for he himself has bought a
house !' . . .

"That other freedman too over there once owned a million but
he's had his losses ; can't call his hair his own now. . . It's pitiful, for what a noble trade he plied ! He was an undertaker and
he used to dine like a king on boars, sweets, fowl ; had chefs and
pastry cooks !" [48]

These miniatures of freedmen are selected out of a
motley crew of many figures in the novel : rhetoricians
and priests, young vagabonds and old roués, wanton
women and corrupt lads, vulgar millionaires and syco-
phantic freedmen, peddlers, and sailors, offended gods and
licentious votaries. The brilliant painting of them all
may perhaps best be seen in the portraits of two leading
figures, Trimalchio and his wife, Fortunata. The whole
character of Trimalchio is drawn with irony : he wishes
to be so splendid ; he appears so ludicrous. He is seen
first off guard, just a bald-headed old man in a red tunic
and sandals playing with a green ball.[49] But he arouses
just as much mirth when he is borne into the banquet in
all his glory, propped up on little pillows, his shaven head
popping out of a crimson robe, heaps of wraps around his
neck and over them all a handkerchief bordered and
fringed. And his jewels ! Rings on his fingers, bangled
bracelet on his arm, a silver tooth-pick in his hand ! [50]
His display of wealth in costume, menu and entertainment is as ostentatious as vulgar. His talk is not restrained by decency. And he would even have played
the buffoon with his hired actor if his wife had not whis-
pered to him that such low fooling did not become his
high position ! [51] His own autobiography is a master-
piece of frank vulgarity. From its first generous admis-
sion to his guests : "I was once just what you are, but I
came to this by my own ability" to his last epigram : "So

[48] *Sat.* 38.   [49] *Sat.* 27.   [50] *Sat.* 32–33.   [51] *Sat.* 52.

your friend who was once a frog is now a king," he exposes his own corruption, venality, industry, shrewdness and megalomania. Losses of fine cargoes by shipwreck only made him build better and bigger vessels. Everything he touched grew like a honeycomb. An astrologer helped him. And under Mercury's protection he built this palace. And then he reels off another proverb : "Have a penny, be a penny : you're valued at what you have." [52]

Such a successful life deserved commemoration in art. So just inside the front door of his palace was a series of frescoes representing Trimalchio's career : first Minerva was leading him into Rome and then came scene after scene with explanatory inscriptions, until at the end of the hall Mercury had him by the chin rushing him to the tribunal of his greatest honor, as Sevir of Augustus, while Fortune with her horn of plenty and the three Fates spinning his golden threads looked on.[53] The little *homunculus* inside his great trappings was never more humorously exposed.

Fortunata is given us in another Franz Hals portrait. This woman from the slums who had been exalted to the skies now measured her money by bushels and enjoyed the use of it. She entered the dining room all dressed in yellow and red, with white and gold shoes. She began at once to take off her jewelry to show her friend, Scintilla, and to announce the value of it. Trimalchio to confirm her boasting had scales brought and the articles weighed ! [54] Yet Fortunata for all her vanity was a sharp-eyed housekeeper and caretaker of Trimalchio's wealth. And he was a henpecked husband if ever there were one, for she had a sharp tongue and could make him believe it was night at noon.[55] Of course they had their differ-

---

[52] *Sat.* 77.   [53] *Sat.* 29.   [54] *Sat.* 67.   [55] *Sat.* 37.

ences, and at times Trimalchio revolted, and showing his teeth, reminded his "viper" of her origin and of her good fortune.[56]   But usually her common sense won the day. Trimalchio's worst threat is that he will not have an image of her put on his tombstone !

Irony in treatment of situations has already been illustrated in the character-sketches.   It usually depends on contrasts or incongruities.   Fortunata has been exalted from the streets to the skies.   Trimalchio's slaves all chant their orders and their replies as if they were actors in a mime.[57]   In the midst of the banquet's magnificence, a jointed silver skeleton is brought in to remind the guests that little man is nothing.[58]   The dinner party ends in a mock funeral.[59]   Giton attempts suicide, but with a blunt razor that makes no wound.[60]   Eumolpus in the shipwreck sits down and writes a poem.[61]   Encolpius was led to a brothel because he foolishly asked an old beldame on the street : "I pray you, mother, do you by any chance know where I live ?" [62]   And of course the most laughable situation of all is the Banquet of Trimalchio.

To have a proper background for this most brilliant part of the *Satyricon* we need to call to mind other famous banquets in Greek and Latin literature and their purpose.   The banquet was a favorite form of both character-drawing and satire.   Indeed among the Latin satirists only Persius seems not to have used it.   The satirical tradition probably started with Menippus.[63]   Here again we must return to Lucian to reconstruct a possible picture of Menippus' *Symposium*.[64]   If Plato's *Symposium* and Lucian's *Carousal* or *The Lapiths* are set side by side,

---

[56] *Sat.* 75.   [57] *Sat.* 31.   [58] *Sat.* 34.   [59] *Sat.* 78.   [60] *Sat.* 94.
[61] *Sat.* 115.   [62] *Sat.* 7.   [63] Athenaeus, xiv. 629 e.
[64] Terzaghi believes that aid for its reconstruction can also be gained from points of agreement among Horace, Petronius and Lucian. N. Terzaghi, *op. cit.*, pp. 107–19.

the juxtaposition emphasizes the vast gulf between the mystic sublimations of Plato and the vulgar ostentation of the Cynic School. The guests at both dinners are philosophers and some of the episodes are the same, but satire has succeeded to sympathetic presentation ; the romance of love between men has been transformed to vice, the battle of beautiful words to brawling insults and fisticuffs over food, Platonic vision to Cynic raillery.

If indeed Lucian as is probable is modelled on a *Symposium* of Menippus, then the Cynic set the satirical coloring for future literary feasts. This in fact is the tradition in Latin satire, both in the Menippean (Varro and Petronius) and in the poetry satire (Lucilius, Horace, and Juvenal) and the same coloring appears in incidental banquet scenes in Apuleius.

The fragments of Varro suggest pictures of both a city banquet and a country meal. Duff describes the first, the *Eumenides* : [65]

"At dinner Cynics and Stoics are played off against each other. An adjournment to go the round of the town gives a chance of testing the Stoic proposition that all men are mad. Galliambics introduce a touch of realism as the inquirers visit the temple of Cybele. Townsfolk are seen to be pursued by the Furies, the third of whom is Madness. The narrator tries to help ; but is haled before 'Current Thought' (*Existimatio*) and entered on the list of the insane. . . Then 'Grey-haired truth' (*Cana Veritas*) comes as a worshipful mistress to console the thinker who has been misunderstood and evilly entreated by the world."

The *Eumenides* was evidently in the Menippean tradition in type of guests, satire, Cynicism.

Aulus Gellius [66] has preserved a record of Varro's country feast in *Nescis quid vesper serus vehat*. Varro wrote

[65] J. Wight Duff, *A Literary History of Rome from the Origins to the Close of the Golden Age*, New York, 1927, p. 336, n. 3.
[66] A. Gellius, *Noctes Atticae*, xiii. 11 ; Buecheler, *op. cit.*, pp. 198–99, I. (333–41), II. (340.)

on the proper number of guests (not less than the Graces, nor more than the Muses) and on the proper conduct of a feast. He said that the banqueters should not be as talkative as those speaking in the forum, nor as silent as if they were in a bedroom ; that conversation should not be on worrying or subtle matters, but pleasant, genial and profitable, with a certain delight from which our natures may become more charming ; this will come about if we talk on matters pertaining to the common use of life which we have no leisure to discuss in the Forum and in business.

In Lucilius,[67] the material from its fragmentary character has to be suggestive rather than descriptive. Many of the fragments are about food and drinks. Various details which reappear in Horace are an offered choice of delicacies, the wiping off the table with a purple cloth, the over-eating of a guest who is stuffed almost to bursting, the picking up a napkin to hide ill-timed laughter.[68] Possibly the fine passage on Virtue, not placed in any book, may come from a philosophical discussion set at a dinner party.[69]

Horace's *Banquet of Nasidienus* [70] is in dialogue form. The host is wealthy and vulgar and is attended by fawning freedmen. The guest of honor is Maecenas who brought with him some satellite friends. A writer of comedies who was present, Fundanius, tells the story to Horace. The conversation was all about food. Mock-heroic style was mingled with colloquialisms. Ludicrous entertainment and episodes interrupt the meal until finally the bored guests escape. In another satire,[71]

---

[67] For Lucilius' life and work, see J. Wight Duff, *op. cit.*, pp. 234–44.
[68] L. R. Shero, "The *Cena* in Roman Satire, *Class. Phil.* xviii (1923), pp. 126–43.
[69] F. Marx, *C. Lucilii Carminum Reliquiae*, Leipzig, 1914, I. 1326–38.
[70] Horace, *Sat.* II. 8.   [71] *Ibid.*, II. 4.

Catius gives Horace a lecture on Gastronomy, so tedious that at the end the poet thanks him ironically for these

vitae praecepta beatae.

Country fare and talk are presented to us in passages which depict life on the Sabine Farm : beans and bacon for food, wine unstinted, conversation not on grand villas or fashionable dancers, but on what makes for happiness, wealth or virtue, the foundations of friendship, the nature of good and of the greatest good. And country neighbors illustrate their faith by fable of country mouse and city mouse.

The freedmen and poor clients who were minor characters in Horace's *Banquet of Nasidienus* assume the leading roles in Petronius and Juvenal. Leaving the novel of the Neronian age till last, let us glance at Juvenal's fifth *Satire.* The theme is the entertainment of a poor client by a wealthy patron and his cruel humiliations. Different wine, water, food and dishes are used for the patron, Virro, and his humble guest. Virro's object is not even thrift, but the production of a comedy or mime of the table with his disappointed client as a butt. Two morals are driven home through all the sorry details ; one for Virro : "Dine with me as with a fellow-citizen ;" one for the client : "Never be the slave of a rich man."

In another satire [72] Juvenal describes a simple country meal where house and dishes match the food, home-grown vegetables, bacon, a fowl, a kid, grapes, pears, apples, all served in earthenware on tables made of native trees. Such a meal was a banquet for senators in early Republican days.

These pictures of elaborate banquets of the vulgar rich and of simple country fare of the contented poor were not

[72] Juv. *Sat.* XI. 56–119.

taken over from satire by Apuleius in his great novel, but in the *Metamorphoses* there are several famous incidental banquet scenes which have influenced both art and literature. Memorable is the dinner in the robbers' cave at which are told the three stories of robber chiefs,[73] the wedding banquet of Cupid and Psyche,[74] the table-talk of the baker's wife at breakfast and dinner,[75] and the picture of the trained ass reclining at table.[76]

One more great work in the banquet tradition is the Greek Menippean satire of Julian, written in the fourth century, the *Symposium* or *Kronia* (Latin *Saturnalia*). At the festival Romulus gave a banquet at which he entertained the gods on the summit of the sky, and the emperor a little lower than the deities, just below the moon. The banquet offered opportunity for character drawing of the Roman Emperors in form of sketches of them as they arrived and the *apologiae* of several who entered a contest set by Zeus for "the best," in which Marcus Aurelius was victor. Here Cynicism brilliantly colors mythology and history.

Through all these banquet satires which preceded or followed Petronius two elements appear : descriptions of externalities, the setting, the food, the wine, various episodes ; and the conversation or set speeches of the guests. In Petronius both elements are brilliantly handled.[77]

The characters of the wealthy parvenu who is host, Trimalchio, of his wife, Fortunata, and their freedmen guests have already been sketched. The service is performed by chanting slaves who personate various char-

---

[73] *Met.* IV. 6–22. [74] *Met.* VI. 24.
[75] *Met.* IX. 15–31. [76] *Met.* X. 15–19.
[77] Other Menippean satires which are not significant for comparison with the *Satyricon* are the *De Nuptiis Philologiae et Mercurii* of Martianus Capella, of the fourth or fifth century, the *Mythologicon* of Fulgentius Planciades, of the sixth century, and Boethius' *De Consolatione Philosophiae*, also of the sixth century.

acters, one Lord Bacchus himself. The dishes are fantastic : a bronze donkey carrying olives in its panniers, a
silver grill, a wooden hen sitting on imitation eggs, a
platter decorated with signs of the Zodiac with appropriate food near each, baskets full of dates hanging from a
wild boar's tusks, waterpots holding oysters, Corinthian
bronzes. A silver dish which has fallen on the floor is,
by the host's orders, swept away with the litter.

Other episodes which diversify the entertainment are
live thrushes released from the wild boar's side, the dance
of Fortunata to the tune of μάδεια, περιμάδεια, the reading of
the accounts and reports of the estate, the acrobats, the
joke-presents for the guests, the real presents of golden
crowns and alabaster bottles of perfume dropped down
on a hoop from the ceiling, the dog-fight of little Mar-
garita and huge Scylax, the stunts of the slaves who imi-
tate birds, trumpeters, mule-drivers, the cook who took
off a tragedian, finally Trimalchio's reading of his own
will and epitaph.

This sad obituary aroused such floods of lamentation
that Trimalchio suggested to cheer up all that they should
adjourn to the bath. There the spectacle of Trimalchio
standing in a bath singing drunken songs while the guests
circled about him in a ring-a-round-a-rosy dance was indeed enlivening. Back again in the dining room, Trimalchio after delivering an oratorical autobiography decided to enact his own funeral. At it the mad blare of
the trumpeters summoned the patrol who thought there
was a fire. Then in the confusion the guests escaped.

The conversation that runs through the labyrinth of
these fantastic episodes is as varied as they are and as
highly colored. Trimalchio indulges in puns, riddles,
literary allusions, would-be learned discussions, indecencies and moral platitudes. The rhetoricians use a

literary style full of rhetorical questions, antitheses, mythological flourishes and theoretical propositions.   The
freedmen's talk is racy, idiomatic, abounding in proverbs,
staccato, open.   The women pursue their sharp, tart way.
Echion, the plain man, warns Professor Agamemnon not
to deride the language of poor people, but to remember
that they know much learning has made him mad.   No
piece of Latin literature affords greater chance for study
of style suited to character.

The subjects are less important than the style.   Many
of them have already been mentioned : education, literary criticism, art, business successes and failures, fortune's
changes, sex indulgence, death and burial.   Ambition
and avarice color much of the talk and set for much of it
the theme that Agamemnon proposed for his *controversia* : "Once upon a time there were a rich man and a
poor man who were enemies."   For the characters in the
novel either once were poor and are now gloating over
their new wealth, or are now poor and are sorrowing over
their losses.   Trimalchio's motto is that of all his guests :

assem habeas, assem valeas ; habes habeberis.[78]

All this description gives little idea of the racy, vulgar
vitality of the *Satyricon,* and comparisons with its predecessors and successors in the field of satire can only
point the way to appreciation.   Collignon [79] has summarized analytically the differences and resemblances between the *Satyricon* and Varro's Menippean satires, between the *Satyricon* and Seneca's *Apocolocyntosis*.   In
all three there is the same mixture of prose and poetry,
the same parody of style of great poets, the same use of
proverbial expressions and popular language, the same
ironic scepticism about tragic myths and about the gods.

[78] *Sat.* 77.   [79] A. Collignon, *Étude sur Pétrone*, Paris, 1892.

Varro's aim was to interest Romans in philosophical studies so he used more moral generalizations. He was also more erudite. Seneca's satire was more personal and violent so that he gave free rein to bitter acerbities.

Collignon goes on to say that the *Satyricon* stands half way between the Menippean satire as seen in the *Apocolocyntosis* and the pure novel as seen in Apuleius' *Metamorphoses*. The *Metamorphoses* is not a Menippean satire, for it contains only four elegiac distichs of an oracle [80] and two lines of a prophetic response given by a Syrian priest.[81] Both the *Satyricon* and the *Metamorphoses* are novels of adventure, admitting various insertions of Milesian tales, epic passages, rhetorical tirades, fantastic stories. Licentious tales are less frequent in Apuleius than in Petronius. Both are colored by irony. There is much more of the marvellous in Apuleius and it is recounted by a writer who is superstitious or at least deeply interested in the supernatural. In Petronius it is ignorant persons who tell tales of witches and werewolves and who believe in them.

Other differences between the two novels are that there is no trace in the *Satyricon* of the sense of religious mystery which concludes the *Metamorphoses*. Second, the *Metamorphoses* could be interpreted as a symbolic story (whether truly or not) ; the *Satyricon* could never be considered symbolic. Again, in Apuleius a horrible realism is often used in tragic or melodramatic tales ; Petronius turns the most tragic situations into comedy. And finally Apuleius often introduces himself in the novel under the name of Lucius and lets his personality appear, while Petronius never appears. [82]

---

[80] *Met.* IV. 33.   [81] *Met.* IX. 8.
[82] Compare B. E. Perry, "Some Aspects of the Literary Art of Apuleius in the *Metamorphoses*," T.P.A.P.A., LIV. (1923), pp. 196–227.

Some reference must be made to the indecencies and obscenities which run through warp and woof of the *Satyricon* and discolor it for the modern reader. To say that Nero's times are not our times is not sufficient explanation. An *elegantiae arbiter* might be expected as an artist to have more discriminating taste in the selection and presentation of material. The real explanation is that Petronius is following an essential feature of the Menippean satire, the Cynic faith and tradition which proclaimed that nothing human was unclean, that all life should be lived openly.

A Cynic love-story which has been preserved shows how far the sage went in the practice of his belief.[83]

Now Crates, the hunch-back, renounced his family, his wealth, his house and lands and adopted the Cynic's wallet and staff, for he had learned that all the riches under the sun were of no aid to living nobly. A girl of high birth and of great wealth fell in love with Crates and scorning all young and rich suitors begged him to marry her. She declared that Crates was everything to her and she threatened her parents that if she were not given to him she would kill herself. When Crates was begged by her father and mother to dissuade the girl, he tried to in every way, but finally he stood before Hipparchia, stripped himself and exposed the hump on his back, laid his cloak, wallet and staff on the ground before her and said to her : "This is the bridegroom. These are his possessions. Look at them and make your choice. For if you are my wife, these will be what you will share."

At once Hipparchia replied that she could find no richer or fairer husband in all the world, and she bade him lead her where he would. The Cynic led her to a portico crowded with people and there in the bright day-

[83] Apuleius, *Flor.* 22 and 14 ; Diog. Laert., VI.

light he lay down and would have made the girl his own
with her consent before the eyes of all if Zeno had not
thrown his robe over them.

Hipparchia never regretted her choice. She too wore
the Cynic's robe and went everywhere with her husband.
At a banquet, Theodorus, the atheist, jeered at her, quoting Euripides,[84]

> "Is this the maid who quitted loom and web ?"

But Hipparchia only replied : "I am she, Theodorus, but
do you think that my decision was wrong when I left the
loom for my education ?"

This story, delicately told by Apuleius and Diogenes
Laertius is an ultimate demonstration of the Cynics' belief in unabashed openness. Petronius himself expresses
their tenets in an epigrammatic poem.[85] It makes little
difference that he quotes as support for his frankness
Epicurus, instead of Crates or Diogenes, for Epicurean
and Cynic teaching merged in theories about wealth, self-
sufficiency, the controlled enjoyment of pleasures of the
body, frankness.

> Why do ye, Catos all, upon me cast
> So stern a look and with it straight condemn
> My little work of new simplicity ?
> The merry charm of my pure speech here laughs
> And its pure tongue reports the people's deeds.
> Who does not know the joys of bed and love ?
> Or who forbids love's fire upon the couch ?
> 'Twas Epicurus, sire of truth, himself
> Who ordered that philosophers should love
> And said that here life won its final crown.

> Quid me constricta spectatis fronte Catones
>   damnatisque novae simplicitatis opus ?
> Sermonis puri non tristis gratia ridet,
>   quodque facit populus, candida lingua refert.

---

[84] Euripides, *Bacchae*, 1236.   [85] *Sat.* 132.

Nam quis concubitus, Veneris quis gaudia nescit ?
  Quis vetat in tepido membra calere toro ?
Ipse pater veri doctos Epicurus amare
  iussit, et hoc vitam dixit habere τέλος.

If I were asked to select pictorial frontispieces for the two extant Latin novels, I should place before Apuleius' *Metamorphoses* a drawing of Lucius, the Ass, with his long ears pricked up inquisitively, as a symbol of the spell of magic cast over much of the novel.   For Petronius' Menippean satire, I should choose a silhouette of the naked Cynic with his wallet and staff, for it is his ironic laughter which runs through the *Satyricon*.

IV

PROSE FICTION IN THE AUGUSTAN AGE: SENECA'S CONTROVERSIAE

In the *Satyricon,* at the banquet of Trimalchio that *nouveau riche* host, would-be patron of all arts and elegance, suddenly asked his guest, Agamemnon, a teacher of rhetoric :

"Do tell me, Agamemnon, what declamation did you deliver in the schools today ?"

When Agamemnon began, "Once upon a time there were a poor man and a rich man, who were enemies," Trimalchio interrupted with : "What is a poor man ?"

"Bravo," said Agamemnon and proceeded to outline some declamation. At once Trimalchio commented : "If this happened, it is not a declamation ; if it did not happen, it is nothing." [1]

This epigrammatic criticism of the practice speeches which were the central core of education in the rhetorical schools might seem fundamental rejection of Roman education by one of the great writers of the first century if we did not remember who is speaking. It is not Petronius, but Trimalchio, and we are left in no doubt as to his qualifications to be a critic. Although he boasts of owning two libraries, one Greek, one Latin, and claims to have a literary education, in his table talk he makes

[1] *Sat.* 48.

Homer write of the twelve labors of Hercules and of how the Cyclops twisted Ulysses' thumb with tongs, has Hannibal fight at Troy, Cassandra kill her children, Daedalus shut Niobe into the Trojan horse, and Agamemnon carry off Helen.   An ignoramus who had profited so little by a literary education could hardly be an intelligent critic of the schools of oratory and their work.

Trimalchio may be taken as a spokesman of all the belittling criticism, ancient and modern, of the system of Roman education in the rhetorical schools.   Traditional comment describes this education as a trivial handling of unrealities, as inadequate preparation for the courts and the cause of the final decline of oratory, as a striving for the novel, the specious and the elaborate in style which destroyed the Atticism of Ciceronian language.   Yet for four or five centuries this was the system of Roman education which held sway and as Edward points out, "its rhetorical quality colours all subsequent literature." [2] In the golden age of Rome, Augustus, Agrippa and Messala went to the schools to hear the speeches of the great teachers.   Asinius Pollio indulged in private exhibitions of his own oratory in declamations.   Ovid, the poet, was made in these schools, and in them all the great writers of the early Empire got their training.   Was there not something more in this education than the futile piffle which Trimalchio denounced ?

To answer this question, I have tried to shape a picture of Roman rhetorical education from ancient sources and its few modern critics and to appraise its value in ancient life.   From Seneca's *controversiae,* from the *declamationes,* major and minor, which go under Quintilian's name, from Petronius, Quintilian, Tacitus, Juvenal and

[2] W. A. Edward, *The Suasoriae of Seneca the Elder,* Cambridge, 1928, Introd. p. xix.

Apuleius, I have culled ideas on education under the *rhetores* which were new to me. And from a few corroboratory sentences in Edward's edition of Seneca's *suasoriae*, Simonds' dissertation on *The Themes Treated by the Elder Seneca*, from Bornecque's masterly monograph, *Les déclamations et les déclamateurs d'après Sénèque le père*, and Boissier's brilliant essay, I believe that I am on the right track.

In these practice speeches of the rhetorical schools, in the discussion of fictitious cases about a poor man and a rich man, about fathers and sons, about cruel step-mothers and raped virgins, about poisoning and kidnaping, the young Romans found the prose fiction and romance of the day and in discussing fictitious cases where unreality let their imagination have full play unhampered by the *mos maiorum,* they developed new psychology, new ethics, new sympathies. The training in *declamationes* involved not merely the art of speaking, but what we should now call ethics or social psychology. And these *declamationes* prepared the way for the Roman novel.

After the Roman boy had been taught by the professors of grammar the correct use of language and the appreciative criticism of poetry and had learned to write paraphrases, ethical sketches and short narratives, he came to the school of the professor of rhetoric to learn the art of public speech. The Roman rhetorical schools which started in imitation of the Greek sophistic methods as early as the second century B.C., had by the age of Augustus gone far from old Cato's conception of the orator as the good man skilled in speaking and of oratory which needed only to acquire a subject to have words follow it. On carefully selected themes and by elaborate processes, skill in delivering a speech for display, a *declamatio,* was developed.

Quintilian outlines the progress in subject matter that a wise teacher will prepare : first historical narratives, then praise of famous men and denunciation of criminals, with the inevitable comparisons of different types of characters, the preparation of commonplaces for decoration, and ethical discussions on such themes as the relative value of town life and country life, or of the professions of the law and the army.[3]

Through this training, preparation was made for two types of formal speeches, the *suasoriae* and the *controversiae*. Edward well defines the *suasoria* as "a fictitious deliberative speech in which the speaker gives advice to a historical or semi-historical character regarding his future conduct" and the *controversia* as "a fictitious speech in an assumed civil or criminal suit." [4] And he also succinctly explains the technical divisions of these speeches : a *sententia* as a "striking or clever expression" used by a *rhetor* anywhere in his speech ; a *divisio* as "a brief summary of the plan of the speech," and the *quaestiones* involved, the *colores* as "the pleas alleged by the accused in explanation or extenuation of his act, or by the accuser to make the accused appear guilty or more guilty." [5] These are the three headings under which Seneca chose to give his reminiscences of the great declaimers in his time.

The *suasoria*, which as the easier type of speech was practiced first by the students, allowed less scope for the imagination. The subjects presented by Seneca are from history and myth : "The three hundred Lacedaemonians sent against Xerxes deliberate whether they should flee as the other contingents had done ;" "Agamemnon deliberates whether he should sacrifice Iphigenia ;" "Cicero

---

[3] *I. O.* II. 4, 18–26.   [4] Edward, *op. cit.*, Introd. p. xxxi.
[5] *Ibid.*, Introd. pp. xxxiv–xxxv.

considers whether he should implore Antony to let him live."

More difficult and more stimulating were the subjects of the *controversiae* and the ancient critics of the rhetorical education are concerned largely with this type of speech. Seneca's ten books of *controversiae*, with their prefaces, although extant only in part, give us a vivid picture of the declamations in the Augustan Age. The questions debated fall under three heads, criminal, civil, social. In the seventy-four cases there are thirty criminal, twenty-six civil and eighteen affecting social status. But, as Duff states : "Many side issues are involved. There are about a score of cases concerning immoral relations such as adultery, seduction, outrage and prostitution : almost as many turn on the disinheriting of children ; seven on poisoning ; seven on tyrants, a theme more at home in Greece. Pirates add a mild flavour of danger to some." [6]

The original sources of the themes are varied. Some were handed down from the Greek rhetorical schools and debated over and over at Rome. Greek and Roman history furnished subjects for the *suasoriae*. Cases about tyrants are concerned with Greek law, not Roman ; and Greek too in origin are cases where the law quoted compels children to support their parents. Stories about pirates were anachronisms since Pompey had cleared the sea. Many cases can be paralleled from actual occurrences in real life recorded by Tacitus.[7] But the majority of the laws cited seem to be fictitious and the treatment purely imaginary. On such themes the young

---

[6] J. Wight Duff, *A Literary History of Rome in the Silver Age from Tiberius to Hadrian*, p. 54.

[7] T. S. Simonds, *The Themes Treated by the Elder Seneca*, Baltimore, 1896, pp. 25–6 ; Edward, *op. cit.*, p. xxxii ; K. v. Morawski, *Wiener Studien*, IV. (1882), pp. 166–68.

students prepared carefully written speeches, pro or con, submitted them to the criticism of their professor, re-wrote them, delivered them before their fellow-students and visitors and finally heard their masters take up the same subjects in model discourses.   What is one to think of such an education ?

Seneca in his prefaces gives us his own ideas of it.   To his most brilliant son, Mela, who hated the thought of public life, he urged : "All the same, pursue the study of eloquence.   For from it the transition to all arts is easy. And it trains those who never practice it." [8]

In another passage he emphasizes the difference be-tween the oratory of the schools and the oratory of the forum : the different audiences, in the schools, pleased hearers, in the forum, critical judges ; the different ob-jects, in the forum, to plead a case, in the schools, to de-claim and as it were to toil in dreams, for this scholastic battle is no real fighting, only a fanning of the air ; the school is a place of sport, the forum an arena.[9]

So one who prepares a declamation writes not to win, but to please.   He chooses flowers of thought instead of arguments.   He indulges in fine writing, for he wishes to gain approbation for himself, not for his cause.   The declaimers invent everything even their adversaries and answer them as they wish and when they wish.   They trade on the indulgence of their hearers, their smiles, their applause, so when they begin to speak in the forum before an unsmiling, critical court, they are discomfited.[10] In the schools, the declaimers, like actors or gladiators, seek beyond all else novelty, for that catches an audience. "Ad nova homines concurrunt, ad nota non veniunt." [11] This effect of novelty is sought by every kind of subtlety and the declaimers learn the art of concealing their in-

[8] *Pref.* II. 3.   [9] *Pref.* III. 12–13.   [10] *Pref.* IX. 1–3.   [11] *Pref.* IV. 1.

genuity.[12]   Often, however, their use of language betrays
their efforts, for those who seek new effects forget that the
tradition of the schools is to use pure diction, not obscure
or archaic words, not obscene or vulgar expressions.   But
an Albucius in his attempt not to seem a scholasticus tries
to vary his style by words of the street and from brilliant
language drops to talk of vinegar, calomel, a buck, a
rhinoceros, latrines, sponges, and other unmentionables.[13]
And this in Seneca's opinion is degradation of the high art
of rhetoric.

Petronius begins his *Satyricon* with a dramatic presentation of two points of view of rhetorical education which
are quite different from Trimalchio's.   Young Encolpius, one of the royster-doyster heroes of the novel, first
airs his criticism and then Professor Agamemnon takes up
a defense of the teachers.   Encolpius declares that schools
do not prepare for the courts, but turn their pupils into
fools, for they do not hear or see anything from everyday
life, rather pirates standing in chains on a shore, tyrants
writing orders that sons shall decapitate their fathers,
oracles in time of pestilence, demanding the sacrifice of
three or four virgins, all described in words sweetened
with honey and seasoned with poppyseed.   Even the style
which the schools teach has lost all modesty and natural
beauty : it is bloated, elephantine, Asiatic.

In reply Professor Agamemnon declares that the teachers are not to blame for these exhibitions : they have to
gibber and squeak with madmen.   Education has to
interest and please very young lads, else there will be no
pupils in the schools.   Teachers are like poor men hunting dinners, fishermen baiting hooks.   The parents are
the ones who are to blame, for they never wish their sons
to endure strict discipline, but hurry them along to the

---

[12] *Pref.* I. 21.   [13] *Pref.* VII. 3.

forum courts as early as possible. They do not see that what pleases lads is not a standard of excellence. And then the Professor is off in a poem about his high calling and an exhortation to all to gird up the soul for such noble labor.[14] Petronius' fictitious schoolmaster has Seneca's ideal for the schools.

Half a century later a genuine professor of rhetoric, Quintilian, in his great treatise on education affirmed that declamation was the most useful of all training if rightly taught. His criticisms take the form of constructive suggestions : first, that the subjects chosen for debate should be as near reality as possible, and that clearly fictitious themes should be treated with the greatest possible verisimilitude. Emotional presentation should be used as preparation for the courts. And realism should be achieved by giving names to characters, by using more complicated plots and words from everyday speech and jests. More details too are desirable : we should know the ages of the characters, their financial status, their parents and children, the strength, the laws and the customs of the cities in which the stories are laid. With such perspicuity does Quintilian insist on improving the vividness of presentation of moot-cases.[15]

The next period of criticism is one of condemnation, for historian and satirist alike deplore the state of rhetorical education. To Tacitus professors of rhetoric teach in schools of impudence and he cannot decide whether the spot itself, the fellow-pupils or the type of studies do more harm. The school inspires no reverence. The audience is composed of youngsters all equally ignorant. The subjects of the declamations are utterly remote from real life, all about rewards of tyrants, fate of ravished girls, remedies for pestilence, immoral mothers. And the style is as debased as the subjects.[16]

In Juvenal the unreality and immorality of the themes of declamations do not excite satire as much as the boredom of monotonous repetition of the same old stuff : cruel tyrant, ravisher, poisoner, wicked and ungrateful husband. This is the cabbage crammed down the teacher's throat again and again *ad nauseam,*

> *occidit miseros crambe repetita magistros.*[17]

The denunciations of Tacitus and Juvenal balance the faith and constructive criticism for this kind of education displayed by Seneca and Quintilian.

But let us leave these ancient critics of Roman rhetorical education and consider now whether from Seneca's *controversiae* we can get first-hand impressions of the effect of the declamations on the young men of the time. If we analyze the types of moot-cases treated, at once it is clear that many are concerned with eternal problems of social life and its ethics, with the inter-relations of members of a family. Marital relations are involved in many cases, which, fictitious though they are, present to us standards of Roman society. I shall illustrate my points by translations of case outlines.

A man who had a beautiful wife left home on business. A foreign merchant who came to the city in his absence three times offered his love to the Lady but she refused it. Presently the merchant died and in his will left all his property to the woman with the eulogy : "I found her chaste." She accepted the inheritance. Her husband on his return from abroad accused her of adultery.[18]

[16] *Dial.* 35.   [17] *Sat.* vii. 150–243.   [18] II. 7.

From the arguing of the case it is clear that not only
Caesar's wife but every Roman matron must be above
suspicion, and that the possibility of a woman holding
property in her own name is obnoxious to the Roman
"Man of Property."

In another case, a wife was tortured by the tyrant of a
city to see whether she knew anything of a plot to kill
him.   Even on the rack she persisted in saying no.   Later
her husband killed the tyrant.   Presently he divorced his
wife because for five years she had borne him no children.
She brought suit against him for ingratitude.[19]   The traditional reason for the duty of matrimony, the rearing of
a family, is urged in the argument.

The husband's culpability was easy to argue in a case
of poisoning.   A man who was proscribed went into exile
accompanied by his wife.   One day she found her husband alone holding a goblet.   When she asked him what
was in it, he confessed that it was poison and that he
wished to die.   She asked to share it.   He drank part
and gave the rest to his wife.   She alone died.   Her will
made her husband her heir.   When he came back from
exile, he was put on trial for poisoning his wife.[20]   Of
course, the damning evidence that is emphasized is the
inheritance.   Shrewd conjectures are made that he had
been studying poisons and had found one in which the
fatal element settled in the bottom of the goblet.

Cases of adultery are common and often involve the
children.   A man had a wife and a daughter by her old
enough to marry.   One day he told his wife whom he had
selected for a son-in-law.   The wife exclaimed : "She
will die before she marries him."   And the daughter did
die before the wedding-day.   Since there were signs of
poisoning, the father tortured a maid who said she knew

[19] II. 5.   [20] VI. 4.

nothing of the poison but his daughter's fiancé had been his wife's lover. The husband brought suit against his wife for poisoning and adultery.[21] The speeches made turned on various possible interpretations of the wife's speech and the value of a slave's evidence under torture.

A more complicated case of adultery involved son and stepson in a murder. A certain man lost his wife by whom he had a son. He married again and had a son by his second wife. When there was constant quarreling between his wife and her stepson, he ordered the young man to leave home. The stepson hired rooms in another part of the house, in fact just the other side of the wall of his father's apartment. Gossip now began to link the matron's name with that of the procurator. One night the father was found killed in his bedroom, his wife wounded, the common wall of the apartments bored through. The relatives asked the five-year-old son who slept with his parents whom he recognized as the murderer. He pointed his finger at the procurator. The elder son accused the procurator of murder, the procurator accused the son of parricide.[22] Here circumstantial evidence and a child's testimony are played off against each other.

Many cases involve more directly the relationship of parents and children. In these the cruel step-mother is a stock character. A man had a son whose mother had died in childbirth. When he married again, he sent the baby boy to the country to be brought up. When his second wife had a son, he sent this boy also to the country. After a long time both were brought back and both were the image of their father so that the living mother could not identify her son. Her husband would not tell her which was hers. She brought action against him for cruelty. The argument for the father maintained that his action was in the children's interest so that both should have a mother and neither a step-mother.[23]

The father as head of the house often tries to control the marriages of his children.   One man had a son and a rich enemy who had a daughter.   While this man was traveling abroad, his death was reported.   His son then married the rich man's daughter.   The father on his return ordered his son to divorce his wife.   When the son refused, his father disowned him.[24]

Another father saved his son's life by arranging a marriage for him.   For when his son was very ill and indeed near death, the doctors pronounced it a mental case. The father went into the sick room with a drawn sword, threatening his son's life if he did not tell him what was on his mind.   The son said he loved his step-mother. The father gave up his wife to him.   For this action, the second son brought a charge of insanity against his father.[25]   Here the conflict of the father's feelings for wife and son was brought out in the speeches.

In another case there is a conflict of duty to father and mother on the part of a son.   A father who had been captured by pirates wrote to his son about ransom.   The son wished to go to ransom his father but his mother who had gone blind from weeping over her loss demanded that he should stay at home to support her and tried to coerce him when he refused to stay.[26]

The young girl as well as the young man figures in these cases, usually in problems of marriage, rape, the status of a Vestal Virgin, suicide.   A simple problem is that of the poor man's daughter whose father had three times refused her hand to a rich man, but was forced by fate to grant it when he and his daughter were ship-

[23] IV. 6.   [24] V. 2.   [25] VI. 7.   [26] VII. 4.

wrecked on the shore of the rich man's estate. The question is : should not the poor man's daughter be allowed a divorce after such compulsion ? [27] Emotional treatment elicited sympathy for the poor and oppressed.

One of the most famous is a case of kidnaping. When a young man had been carried off by pirates, his father refused to ransom him. The daughter of the chief of the gangsters told the youth that she would help him escape if he would marry her. The flight was successful, and the young man kept his word. His father, now having found a suitable *parti* for his son in a rich orphan girl, ordered his son to divorce the pirate's daughter and marry the heiress. He refused. His father disowned him.[28] Here was a chance for ingenious support of father on the ground of social position and of son on the ground of gratitude and honor. The discussion of social status is significant.

An illustration of extreme exercise of the old Roman *patria potestas* over life and death is a war-time story. In a civil war, a family was divided in allegiance, and a young wife found her father and brother on one side and her husband on the other. She followed her husband. After her side was conquered and her husband killed, she returned to her father. When he would not receive her into his house, she asked : "How do you wish me to satisfy you ?" He answered : "Die." She hanged herself before the door of her home. The father was accused by his son of dementia.[29]

Cases of rape are argued under a fictitious law which permitted a raped girl to choose between the death of her assailant or marriage to him without dowry. A father condemned for murder went into exile. His daughter was attacked. The ravisher went to her father, persuaded him to order his daughter to choose marriage and got him to write a letter to that effect to his son.   On the son's advice, however, the girl chose the death of the assailant.   When the father came home, he disowned his son.[30]

One version of the law was that the ravisher had to die within thirty days if he did not win over his own father and the girl's.   A certain man won over the girl's father but not his own.   He accused his father of insanity.[31]

A shift of choice on the part of the girl made a psychological situation for discussion.   A raped girl chose marriage.   The man accused said he had not raped her. When he was convicted, he wished to marry her.   The girl then begged free choice.[32]

The standard of purity demanded by society from Vestal Virgins is attested by several cases.   In one a Vestal wrote a single line of poetry :

> Happy are brides.   May I die if the
> married life is not blissful.

She was tried for incest.[33]

In another case, a Vestal judged guilty of incest, was cast down from the Tarpeian Rock, but lived.   An attempt was made to have the punishment repeated.[34]

Another case, based on an historical occurrence,[35] introduces a character conspicuous in Roman society and in Roman comedy, the meretrix.   A courtesan at a dinner given by the proconsul Flamininus remarked that she had never seen a man beheaded and begged her host to grant her that spectacle.   Flamininus had a condemned prisoner brought in and decapitated to gratify the woman.

[30] IV. 3.   [31] II. 3.   [32] VII. 8.   [33] VI. 8.   [34] I. 3.
[35] Livy XXXIX. 42 ; Valerius Maximus II. 9, 3 ; Plutarch, *Flamininus*, c. 18 ; Cicero, *De Senectute*, 12.   In some of these narratives the favorite of Flamininus is a boy.

He was accused of *lèse majesté*.[36]   The corruption, heart-lessness and callousness of the woman who demanded this favor are ruthlessly exposed.   And sympathy for the criminal elicits a speech full of compassion in which the emotions of the condemned man are portrayed : his sud-den hope on being called to the dinner that he is to be pardoned ; his outraged pride when he is to be butchered to make a Roman holiday.

The same types of cases appear in the two collections of *Declamationes* which have come down under Quintilian's name.   J. Wight Duff has well summarized the themes : Of the collection of nineteen fairly long productions, he says : "Some turn upon immorality or crime ; some have a public bearing : more often, with features akin to the Greek comedy of manners or a modern novel, their interest is social or domestic.   A few could be served up as romances like *The Philtre of Loathing* (xiv, xv), or as spiritualistic cases for investigation by the Psychical Re-search Society, like *The Spell-bound Tomb* (x), in which a mother, hitherto comforted by visions of her dead son, is aggrieved because a magician, at her husband's instiga-tion, has by enchantment cut off communication with the ghost.   A detective story might be made out of *The Wall with Handprints of Blood* (i) ; and then we have the usual quota of pirates.   A half-romantic theme like a wizard's prophecy may be entangled with two imaginary laws which create a dilemma for debate." [37]

Of the 145 shorter declamations (from a collection originally numbering 388), Duff writes that they "are more profitably represented in specimens than in their wearisome total.   The problems are such as arise out of cases of outrage, divorce, adultery, murder of or by out-laws, tyrannicide, military desertion, shipwreck, prodigality of sons, harshness of fathers, or (like later Italian *novelle*) marriage between a son and a daughter of hostile families. Handling the type of theme already worn threadbare in Augustan days,[38] they cannot be considered uniformly entertaining. Yet there are exceptions, and all is not monotony. One may even be grateful for absurd instances with outlines that might serve for wildly impossible tales ; and, dipping further into the collection, one cannot deny that it has some variety." [39]

Themes in the Pseudo-Quintilian, not found in Seneca, are the use of magic [40] cited by Duff, the use of science, and an elaboration of motives of treason and fidelity. The use of science appears in a case discussing the relation of parents to children.[41] Twin babies fell sick. The doctors said they had the same disease. When the others gave them up, one doctor said he would cure one if he might inspect the vital organs of the other. With the consent of the father, he operated on one child, who died. The other was cured. The father was accused of cruelty by the mother.

A case of treason involving hostile families is told in number xi. A poor man and a rich man were enemies. Each had three sons. Their state had a war. The rich man was elected general and departed to camp. A rumor spread that he was betraying the state and in an assembly the poor man accused him of treason. The result was that in his absence his sons were stoned to death by the people. The rich man came back from the war victorious. He demanded the sons of the poor man for punishment. Their father offered himself but the rich man refused, for there were laws that a traitor should be

---

[38] For parallels of the subjects of the *Controversiae* of Seneca, the Declamations of the Pseudo-Quintilian and Calpurnius Flaccus, see Simonds, *op. cit.*, pp. 71–81.
[39] J. Wight Duff, *op. cit.*, p. 418.   [40] X.   [41] VIII.

punished by death and that a slanderer should suffer the same fate as the accused if he should be convicted.

Another case of hostile families, one rich, one poor, is much more elaborate in plot and illustrates well the complications devised in some of these longer declamations of the Pseudo-Quintilian.

A poor man and a rich man who were enemies each had a son. The young men were friends. The son of the rich man was seized by pirates and wrote his father about ransom. When the father delayed action, the son of the poor man set out to do something. He found that his friend was not with the pirates, but had been sold to the head of a troupe of gladiators. He arrived at the state where a gladiatorial show was taking place just when his rich young friend was going to fight. He was able to make an agreement with the giver of the games that he might ransom his friend by taking his place. He begged from his friend that he would support his own poor father should he be in need. Then he was killed in the combat. The son of the rich man on returning home found the poor man in great need. He began to support him openly. His own father disowned him.[42]

I have quoted these cases to suggest how much chance they afforded for psychological character study, emotional appeal, and establishment of ethical principles. Even so brief a review of typical moot cases shows the problems being discussed in the rhetorical schools : the standards of morality and etiquette demanded of Roman matrons, the young girl's position in society, conditions of her marriage or of her becoming a Vestal Virgin, the extent of the control of a *pater familias* over the lives and liberty of his sons and daughters, questions of property-holding, avarice, ransom, the conception of slavery, suicide, mur-

[42] IX.

der.   The very nature of these questions is so eternal, so modern that I cannot agree with the traditional criticism of Roman education that it was "ridiculously remote from real life," [43] dull in stultifying repetitions, or pernicious in lowering moral standards.   Rather under the guise of preparation for oratory it presented for thoughtful consideration and individual presentation fundamental problems of society and ethics, of psychology and of romance.   This point can be illustrated by a detailed study of some of the speeches made in individual cases in Seneca's *Controversiae.*

One is the case of the young woman who wished to become a Vestal after she had been kidnaped, sold to a *leno,* placed in a brothel, tried for murder and acquitted. The weight of the argument is against the girl.[44]   The law quoted is : "Let a priestess be chaste of the chaste, pure of the pure."   The girl's story was that whenever a man came to her room in the brothel, she begged at once for her proper fee without service, and all respected her appeal, until a certain soldier offered her violence.   Him she killed.

Latro, Seneca's favorite rhetorician, tried to break down from circumstantial evidence and the probabilities the truth of the girl's story that she has never lost her virtue. He does not know what befell her among the pirates, but he knows what might have happened.   Her claim for chastity is : "I killed a soldier."   But she did not kill the procurer.   She was taken to the brothel, given a small bedroom.   Her price was fixed.   A notice was put up over her door.   Even if no one raped her, all came to rape her and left as if they had.   Moreover she committed murder.   Suppose someone had met her when she escaped, all blood-stained.   And then Latro in an impassioned peroration finally attacked the girl's character : "If your Mother had been a prostitute, it would injure you now. On account of you, I would not give a priesthood to your children."

Marullus instead of using the factual narrative which Latro employed, discredited the girl's story by suggestive irony. Her very charm is so seductive that we may know she has been in a house of prostitution ; we may know too that she has lived among pirates, because her hands are stained with blood. She claims : "No one touched me." The *leno's* accounts prove she was in his house. Of the men who paid their fees to her, let us suppose that a violent man entered her room, or a lusty fellow, or a man armed with a sword.

Vinicius showed more human sympathy and was willing to admit the truth of the story, but with horror he brought out the impossibility of associating even doubtful reputation with a holy priesthood. The gods judge the conscience of each. We have to judge what we see. We have seen what you have done openly. The gods know the rest. I would call you unworthy of the priesthood if you had stepped over the threshold of a brothel.

For this woman shall a *lictor* make a way through the crowd ? To her shall the consuls give the *imperium* ? Why, she will pardon every meretrix !

A priestess ought not to have a maid like you. The facts of your life are these : you stood naked on the shore for the inspection of a purchaser ; a pirate sold you, a procurer bought you, a brothel received you. The only honorable escape for you from the house of prostitution was suicide. I pity you, but we do not make those we pity priestesses.

Cestius expressed in an epigram the general sentiment : "You a maiden stood in a brothel. Granted that no one violated you, the place itself violated you." He declared brutally that probably she had always been corrupt and that the reason her family did not ransom her was because they hated her.

The defense for the girl was very slight. Fuscus sententiously declared : "The gods have produced a miracle : liberty for a captive girl, chastity for a prostitute, innocence for an homicide." Latro offered : "There have been captives who were more fortunate, none who were braver." Marullus dared to say that the girl's purity was her actual defense. "Say that all went in as to a prostitute, but came out as if from a priestess." Triarius emphasized the gratitude of the girl to the gods to whom she dedicates the virginity which she owes to them. There were not lacking those who hurled obscenities against her.

Conspicuous in the treatment of the case are the vivid narrative of the plain facts, the defamation of character on the ground of probabilities, the dramatic contrast between the house of the prostitutes and the House of the Vestals. The emotional coloring varies from irony and indignation to a mystic belief in purity and a religious exaltation over the protection of the gods.

In the case of the suicide pact between husband and wife, the speeches turn not on any moral principles or religious scruples, but rather on the ingenuities of the rhetorician's art. Under the pact, the husband sent a false report of his death to his wife. She threw herself down from some high place, but lived. Ordered by her father to leave her husband, she refused. Her father then disowned her.[45]

Seneca points out that no subtle plan (*divisio*) is neces-

45 II. 2.

sary in the case, for there are simply two questions : first,
can a father disown a daughter because of her marriage ;
second, what are the ethics involved in the pact and oath ?
The speeches which he quotes are concerned largely with
the last.   They discuss whether lovers' oaths are legally
binding ; whether the intent of the husband was evil or
not ; and they set off brilliant pyrotechnics on the lady's
great love.   The devotion of the pair is expressed in dialogues in which they vie with each other to prove whose
love is greater.   And the wife declares she wishes to win
the great glory of heroines of old who immolated themselves on husbands' pyres or saved their husbands' lives
by dying in their stead.

Hispo emphasized the devotion which was the keynote
of the lady's life : her oath was in her father's name, "So
may I please my sire !"   She can no more live without
her father than without her husband.

Against such encomia Latro protested for the father
that even if the husband had no evil intent, and was
simply testing his wife, never believing that she would
die, she should not be left with so rash and unwise a character.   Moreover the husband's motives are open to very
serious suspicion.

Hispo Romanus in a second speech quoted did not
adopt so serious a tone, but declared that the oath had
been a jest and the husband, forgetting their suicide pact,
had sent the message to see whether his wife's love had
lasted.   The wife knew the news was false and threw herself down from a place where she could not perish in
order to frighten her husband with false news as he had
her.   The whole episode was jest against jest.

The most interesting part of the defense to us is the
speech which the poet Ovid made when he was a boy at

the school of Arellius Fuscus.   Usually Seneca reported
the speeches of famous rhetoricians.   His favorite speaker
was Latro who would never even listen to the declamations of young students in the schools, but would only
deliver model speeches for them.   Ovid's later fame ap-
parently made Seneca interested in reporting one of his
practice speeches as a lad.   Seneca says that Ovid used a
very different kind of oratory from Latro's : his genius
was polished, appropriate and lovable.   His oratory indeed seemed prose poetry.   In this case he used more
ingenuity than any of the others did, but he observed no
order in his points, in fact he disliked argument and for
this reason rarely declaimed *controversiae* and only on
ethical subjects.   The excerpts from Ovid's declamation
on the suicide pact might except for the form be quotations from his *Heroides.*

The whole difficulty lies in this, that you grant that
husband and wife love each other.   You must permit
them to take oath, if you permit them to love.

The husband says : "What oath do you think we
made ?   Your name was holy to us.   If we proved false,
she invoked her father's anger, I my father-in-law's.
Spare us, father.   We did not swear falsely."

The father complains that anyone is more dear to his
daughter than he is.   Great heavens, how did he love his
wife ?

He loves his daughter and disowns her.   He grieves
that she is in danger and takes her away from the man
without whom she declares she cannot live.   He complains of danger to her whom he almost lost.   He bids
her love cautiously !

It is easier to set an end to love, than a measure.   Will
you force lovers to observe bounds which you approve, to
do nothing except after careful consideration, to make no

promises except those which they expect to keep under oath, to weigh their words in the scales of reason and loyalty? So old men love!

You have known only a few of our sins, father. Often we have quarreled and made up, and, what you believe impossible, we have sworn falsely. What concern of a father are lovers' oaths? Believe me, they are not even the concern of the gods.

You, my wife, are not to be self-satisfied as though you were the first woman who has sinned so. One lady died with her husband, another died for her husband. Yet every age will honor them, every great writer will celebrate them. Endure your good fortune, my father-in-law. How little value in your eyes has the great deed!

For the future, as you command, we have been made more careful. We confess our error. We had forgotten when we took oath that there was a third who loved more. Ye gods, so may it be always!

You are adamant, my father-in-law? Take your daughter. I who sinned deserve punishment. Why should I be the cause of disgrace to my wife, of bereavement to her father? I will leave the state. I will flee, I will go into exile. In whatever way I can, I will bear my longing with patience, a remedy pitiable and cruel. I would die if I were able to die alone.

With such ardor for passion, such irony for aged caution, with such rhetorical questions, antitheses and *reductio ad absurdum* did Ovid when a lad plead the rights of love's art.

My third case, which involves the manumission and marriage of a slave, is significant for the picture of class distinctions in society and of the position of slave and freedman. In a certain city, a tyrant who had seized the power permitted slaves to kill their masters and rape their

mistresses.   The leaders of the state fled, among them
one who had a son and daughter.   His slave, when all the
other slaves had raped their mistresses, saved the daughter
of his master.   After the tyrant was killed, the exiles returned and crucified their slaves.   The father of the
faithful servant manumitted his and gave him his daughter in marriage.   He was accused of insanity by his son.[46]

The arguments used against the father in most of the
quoted speeches are the social status of the slave-husband
and the impossible family situation created by the marriage : the relatives of the husband are among those crucified for rape ; the bridegroom's slave-partner was turned
out of her bed in the slave's cell that her mistress might
take her place ; the children of this marriage will be de-
classed.

Besides this, wrong has been done the slave : a good
servant has been turned into a criminal ; his self-restraint
has been destroyed.   But perhaps all along he was design-
ing and saved his mistress for himself ; or prudence directed his self-control since he feared execution when the
tyrant was overthrown.

The girl's fate is more tragic than that of the other
women : their wrongs are over ; they can contract other
marriages.   She is doomed forever.

Asinius Pollio put in the mouth of the brother the
deepest humiliation :

"In the fescennine verses at the wedding men joked about a
cross for the bride-groom.   What misery I suffered on the day
when the republic began to be enslaved !   What misery on the
day when I went into exile !   And what misery on my sister's
wedding-day !

"Pitiable sister, perhaps you have step-children who are little
house-slaves.

[46] VII. 6.

"Father, I wish to marry. To which one of your slave-women will you betroth me?"

The arguments for the defense of the slave are less emotional and more ethical. Varius Geminus plead that great men had often married freedwomen : Cato married the daughter of his farmer. Someone may retort : "But she was free-born." I answer : "But he was Cato. There is more difference between you and Cato than between a freedman and a farmer." And then he adds another argument which is rather amusing : How many advantages a subject and humble husband would have ! The wife will not fear bad temper, reproaches, a rival, a divorce. The father will always have his daughter at home. And be it remembered that the slave did a noble deed.

Albucius spoke as a philosopher urging that by nature no one is free, no one is a slave. It is chance that has bestowed these names on us in the course of time. We too once were slaves. Remember King Servius Tullius.

Silo Pompeius pleaded that an economic reason caused the marriage : the father had no dowry to give because he lost all under the tyrant.

Argentarius said the girl wished the marriage and seemed to favor the slave as indeed she should.

Gavius Sabinus had the father lower his own dignity and confess that his own rank was humble so that he was at a loss to whom to marry his daughter ; he thought he must seek some freedman and preferred a man he knew, whose affection to his family was proved. He declared that he knew if he himself died, his daughter would be safe with her husband and that for his part he did not despise a man who had despised the orders of a tyrant.

Now although this is a fictitious case and the so-called

tyrant did not exist in Italy, where in literature can we find a more vivid transcript of social conventions, family pride, and revolt against parental control? Here too is voiced the Stoic teaching that real slavery is determined not by outward condition, but by inner spirit. And here romance is hinted by one bold young orator who thinks the young girl may have fallen in love with her savior. The character-drawing of the conventional, proud, indignant brother is good. The father appears now as a shattered insane old man, now as an humiliated, poverty-stricken refugee, now as an unworldly idealist. And the young girl is described once as a tragic, disgraced and reluctant bride, and again as a grateful and affectionate creature, willing to be the reward of nobility. Psychology and ethics shaped these declamations.

Suppose that in any one of these cases Quintilian's recommendations for greater realism of treatment should be observed : that names should be given to all the characters, and their family and financial status should be more clearly defined ; that local color should be added by description of the scenes of the stories ; that plots should be more complicated and more details of action should be given, that more colloquial language should be used. A writer who would adopt Quintilian's suggestions could easily make a *novella* out of any one of the three cases whose treatment I have just described. Great human elements in characters and situation are already present. Motivation has been suggested ; dialogue has been introduced. And the oratorical presentation could easily be transformed to melodrama or romance.

I have tried by this analysis to show how near to fiction the declamations of the rhetorical schools were. Character drawing was attempted by illuminating presentation and by contrasting types. Realistic narrative of events provided setting. Direct dialogue enlivened narrative. Emotional coloring enhanced interest by arousing pity and awe, or by displaying irony and humor. And a deeper significance was attached to the case by a philosophical discussion of the conventions of society, the nature of morality and the ethics of action. The greatest value of Roman education under the *rhetores* was not the training for oratory, but the stimulus to the imagination given by discussion of human beings and their problems.

The influence of the declamations of the schools on the two extant Roman novels is striking. We have already seen that in the *Satyricon* professors of rhetoric are among the characters and a discussion of education in the rhetorical schools opens the novel. The speech of Hermeros, fellow-freedman of Trimalchio, at the banquet is a remarkably lively and vituperative declamation of a natural orator who boasts that he never studied geometry, criticism and poetry but learned from a stern schoolmaster, life, how to exist, earn and talk.[47] And in the adventure on the boat, two sides of the case of the disguised young men and the skipper are argued by Eumolpus and Lichas in the best declamatory style.[48] The very character of the *Satyricon* as a novel of common life with its low characters, its crass realism, its vulgarities of thought and speech may be regarded as a revolt against the elegant fictions of the schools which Encolpius attacks so lustily.

In the picaresque novel of Apuleius, both the discursive style, the Asiatic coloring and the many oratorical speeches delivered by the characters show the sophist's art of which the author was a professor and master. There is peculiar irony in having Lucius the ass, "philosophizing" as he says, deliver one diatribe on the malignity of

[47] *Sat.* 58–59.   [48] *Sat.* 107.

Fortune who giveth her wealth to the wicked and the unworthy [49] and another on the venality of all lawyers and judges, those "vultures in togas." [50]   Moreover, one famous scene in the *Metamorphoses* might have been transferred from the rostra of a school of rhetoric.   I refer to the trial of Lucius for murder.[51]

The hero on returning late at night and drunk to the house of his host Milo saw three great figures at the door whom he believed thieves.   To anticipate their robbery and violence, he ran each through with his sword and so to bed.   The next morning he was haled to court, accused of murder of the three and put on trial.   Lucius' eloquent speech of defense might have been composed by any young orator of the schools.   He declares that he is a murderer yet innocent in intent.   He prevented murder by murder.   He heard the three thieves planning violent entrance of Milo's house, slaughter of all within and robbery.   He felt it was his duty as a good citizen to prevent such outrage.   When he attacked them, he nearly lost his own life in the struggle with each of them. And he described his battles in detail.   Such self-defense, such protection of a host deserve reward, not execution. His life has always been upright.   These three men were strangers to him so his murders were not caused by personal enmity or hope of gain.

As Lucius sat down weeping piteously at his own plight, he was outraged to find that all the courtroom was rocking with laughter — a strange response to his appeal. Then a woman is mourning carrying a baby and an old woman in rags came in and stood beside the bier demanding justice in the name of slain husbands and fatherless child.   And the aged judge proposed to extract the truth from the malefactor by the rack.   But first the old

[49] *Met.* VII. 2.   [50] *Met.* X. 33.   [51] *Met.* III. 1–12.

woman demanded that the murderer be forced to un-
cover the bodies that all might behold her beautiful sons
who had been so foully murdered. The horror-stricken
hero as he uncovered the bier, beheld not three corpses,
but three great wine-skins, all gashed in the very places
where he thought he had wounded robbers !

At this the laughter at the battle with the wine-skins
broke out afresh and the crestfallen Lucius found it was
all a mock trial staged to amuse the public at the annual
festival of Risus, the God of Laughter, and his eloquent
oration had been delivered for a fictitious case to entertain the world. It is only later that Lucius' humiliation
over the hoax is assuaged by learning that the goatskins
at the door had been animated by a mistake in the magic
operations of Pamphile [52] so that he had after all fought
with living creatures. This transformation clearly
played a part in interesting the hero in magic art. The
Risus Festival with the courtroom scene has been shown
by Prof. B. E. Perry to be one of Apuleius' additions to
the original Greek tale.[53] This courtroom scene is a
significant link between the presentation of imaginary
cases in the schoolroom and the development of fiction in
the romantic novel.

I hope that I have given enough evidence to demon-
strate the grounds of my belief that in the declamations of
the schools lay the prose fiction of the Augustan Age, and
that these *controversiae* helped prepare the way for the
Latin novel. Certainly, I think, Petronius and Apuleius
were aware of the relation of *controversiae* to fiction.
Later ages confirm this hypothesis of the value of the
declamations for the development of fiction. The chief

[52] *Met.* III. 16–18.
[53] B. E. Perry, "On Apuleius' *Metamorphoses* II, 31–III, 20," *A. J. P.*, xlvi
(1925), pp. 253–62. For another interpretation of the Risus episode, see
D. S. Robertson, "A Greek Carnival," *J. H. S.*, xxxix (1919), pp. 110–15.

source of the mediaeval *Gesta Romanorum* was Seneca's *controversiae*.[54]   Later Mlle. de Scudéry used the plot of the pirate's daughter [55] in her romance *Ibrahim ou l'illustre Bassa*.   And a wealth of unused plots lie in the storehouses of the declamations of Seneca and the Pseudo-Quintilian.

My review of the material in Seneca has convinced me that Bornecque is right in saying that here in the rhetorical schools the first drafts were made of a new literary genre, the romance.

"Les sujets sont extraordinaires, les sentiments exceptionnels ? Mais n'est-ce pas à cette circonstance que nous devons de trouver, dans les Controverses, l'ébauche d'un genre qui, jusque là, n'existait pas à Rome, et pour lequel on ne rencontre à aucune époque, dans la langue latine, un terme précis et spécial, du roman, roman d'amour où l'homme respecte la femme, 'la traite presque comme une égale, et, quand il l'aime, la fait monter jusqu' à lui,' [56] tableaux de moeurs, ou, tout simplement, récits d'aventures singulières qui naissent d'incidents étranges et de complications imprévues." [57]

[54] *G. R.*, C. 2 (*Cont.* I. 2) ; 3 (I. 3) ; 4 (I. 5) ; 5 (I. 6) ; 6 (II. 2) ; 7 (II. 4) ; 14 (VII. 4) ; 73 (III. 1) ; 90 (VI. 3) ; 100 (I. 4) ; 134 (IV. 4) ; in L. Friedländer, *Roman Life and Manners under the Early Empire*, New York, 1913, vol. IV. pp. 297–8.

[55] *Cont.* I. 6.

[56] Collignon, "La Littérature Romanesque chez les Latins," *Annales de l'Est*, 1898, p. 344.

[57] Henri Bornecque, *Les Déclamations et les Déclamateurs d'après Sénèque le père*, Lille, 1902, p. 130.

V

APULEIUS' ART OF STORY-TELLING

THE novel of Apuleius called the *Metamorphoses* is unique in Latin literature. It is the one complete Latin novel extant. It is entirely different from the fragmentary *Satyricon* in style, theme and scope. It is linked to the Greek novels that were being written in the same period only by general plot and by the tales of adventure which it shares with them. It deserves special study as a novel because of its own brilliancy and because of its position in the history of fiction. Apuleius' preface to the Reader presents its greatest claim for consideration, its entertaining character : *lector intende ; laetaberis.*[1]

In the same preface Apuleius himself states the sources of his novel. It is a Greek story. In it various Milesian tales are woven together. Paper and pen are Egyptian. Its theme is the transformation of human beings into different shapes and their retransformations to themselves. The language is an exotic and rhetorical Latin learned by a foreigner who had acquired Greek first. The story is told in the first person by the hero, Lucius, directly to the reader who is to be entertained by it. Modern scholarship has only proved and expanded the truth of these autobiographical statements.

[1] For an account of the life and writings of Apuleius see E. H. Haight, "Apuleius and his Influence," *Our Debt to Greece and Rome*, New York, 1927.

The plot is simple. The hero Lucius who is greatly interested in magic is enabled by the aid of the maid-servant of a witch to achieve transformation. But a mistake in the use of the unguents changes him not into a bird as he had planned, but into an ass. Although he knows that the antidote is a meal of roses, he is kept by Fortune from securing release through long months and meets various adventures until at last through the aid of the goddess Isis Lucius the Ass becomes again Lucius the Man.

The general outline of this plot is taken from a Greek story. Included in the writings of Lucian is a Greek novelette with the title Λούκιος ἢ ὄνος which has the same outline as the *Metamorphoses,* the transformation of a man into an ass and his adventures in that shape. Another Greek version of the same story is known from a reference in Photius to the *Metamorphoses* of Lucius of Patrae,[2] and it seems probable that Lucian wrote the lost *Metamorphoses* and that his work was the common source of the extant Λούκιος ἢ ὄνος and of Apuleius' *Metamorphoses.* But the inter-relation of these three works must be hypothetical and we are concerned now only with a comparison of the two extant stories, one in Greek, one in Latin, with the same general plot.

The most noticeable and striking difference is in the endings, for the great final book of the *Metamorphoses* on the aid of Isis and her worship has no counterpart in Λούκιος ἢ ὄνος. There the retransformation occurs at an obscene exhibition. In Apuleius the ass escapes from such an exhibition, has a vision of Isis and is saved by her. Moreover, the central, the longest and the most famous tale in Apuleius, the love story of Cupid and Psyche, is not found in Λούκιος ἢ ὄνος nor indeed in literature before

[2] *Bibl. Cod.* 129, Migne.

Apuleius related it.   Besides these two great additions
to the Greek story there appear in Apuleius many short
stories of the Milesian type and of other types which are
not in the Greek version.   Indeed the originality of the
Latin writer is seen most clearly in a comparison of the
Metamorphoses with the Greek novelette on the same
theme.

To appreciate the narrative art of Apuleius it is necessary first not only to review the outline of his plot, but
to understand the character of his hero, to study the major
short stories (*novelle*) interwoven with the plot and the
use of incidental stories to advance it, and from all these
to get a conception of the technique of the successful raconteur and the themes underlying his work.

The hero Lucius who recounts this *ich-roman* is out
for adventure, is full of mental curiosity, avid of experience, eager to know life, cities and men.   He is interested
in human beings of all classes and conditions, their relation to each other, to the universe about them, to the
unseen forces which condition their lives.   He has much
sympathy for the poor and the oppressed.   He feels that
animals are very near human beings and share their
struggles and sufferings.   And in his narrative certain
recurring themes betray not only Lucius' interests, but
Apuleius' : adventure, tyranny, sex, magic, folk-lore and
religion.   Author and hero finally become completely
identified in retransformation and reinterpretation of
life's problems, when Lucius the Greek is suddenly called
"a poor man of Madaura," and experiences the many ini-
tiations into mystic cults in which Apuleius himself had
participated.[3]

The stories which Lucius tells are varied in time, length,
setting, characters, patterns.   Since there seems to be a

[3] *Apol.* C. 55.

possible design in their arrangement, it will be well to analyze in their sequence the fifteen major stories that diversify the plot and then summarize the incidental stories which are used to develop it.   For convenience in reference I will at once list the fifteen *novelle* which seem to me of major importance, giving them titles which will facilitate future identification.

1. Socrates and the witch Meroe, I. 5–20.
2. Thelyphron and the witches, II. 20–31.
3. The battle of the wineskins, II. 32–III. 18.
4. ⎫
5. ⎬ Stories of robber chieftains, IV. 6–22.
6. ⎭
7. The kidnaped bride, Charite, ⎰ IV. 23–27.
   ⎨ VI. 25–VII. 14.
   ⎱ VIII. 1–15.
8. The love-story of Cupid and Psyche, IV, 28–VI. 24.
9. The lover under the tub, IX. 5–7.
10. The baker's wife, ⎫
11. The sandals under the bed, ⎬ IX. 11–31.
12. The fuller's wife, ⎭
13. Rich man, poor man, IX. 33–38.
14. The amorous step-mother, X. 2–12.
15. The murderess of five, X. 23–28.

The transformation of Lucius into the ass comes early in the narrative between stories 3 and 4, III. 21–25.   The narrative of the retransformation is the real theme of the whole final book, the eleventh.   Against this framework, let us proceed to consider the individual stories.

The story of Socrates and the witch Meroe [4] is told by a traveler, Aristomenes, to two fellow-travelers as they ride up a long hill in Thessaly.   It is told as a personal adventure and the narrator identifies himself as a food merchant from Aegina.   In the course of a business trip

4 *Met.* I. 5–20.

he encountered an old friend, Socrates, who was in such a pitiable state that he looked like a ghost or a beggar. Aristomenes after clothing and feeding him discovered he was in the toils of a terrible witch. Socrates described her powers by such vivid illustrations that Aristomenes himself was terrorized, and urged his friend after a night's rest to flee with him early in the morning.

They had hardly gone to sleep when the doors burst open miraculously, Aristomenes' bed was turned upside down on top of him and two witches entered who from their chatter were found to be Meroe, the mistress of Socrates, and Panthia. After deciding not to chop up Aristomenes but to let him live to bury his friend, Meroe plunged a knife into the neck of the sleeping Socrates, caught the blood in a little receptacle, put her hand down through the wound and dragged his heart out, stuffed a sponge into the cut, bade it never to cross running water and then was off with her companion. The doors of their own accord crashed shut behind them.

Aristomenes in utter terror, sure that he would be arrested in the morning for murdering his companion, tried to rouse a drowsy ostler and make him unbar the stable door so that he could get his horse and ride away. When the ostler refused because robbers were abroad at night, Aristomenes attempted to hang himself with a rope from the bed, but the rope being old and rotten broke and let him down on Socrates. To his amazement Socrates at once woke up just as the ostler entered to call them both.

So everything was changed. Aristomenes believed he had had a nightmare. Socrates related another horrible dream of having his throat cut and both rode off in high spirits. But when they sat down for breakfast under a plane-tree, Socrates began to grow very pale as he ate and

Aristomenes, watching him, felt all his terror returning. And when Socrates knelt down by the river to drink, suddenly the sponge fell out of his neck, the wound reopened, and there he died. Aristomenes could only bury him and flee in terror to a country where no one knew him or could accuse him of murder. So he had come to Aetolia in voluntary exile and there had married a new wife.

At the end of the story the two fellow-travelers discussed its credibility and Lucius in answer to the scepticism of the other declared he believed every word of it, for life is full of just such marvels. Indeed the effect of credibility has been produced on the reader by the realism of minute details in the descriptions, the vivacity of the conversations between Aristomenes and his ruined friend Socrates, between the two witches, between Aristomenes and the drowsy ostler, above all by the character drawing of Socrates and the witch Meroe. Touches of humor where Aristomenes begs Socrates not to rant like a tragic actor and even in his terror under the bed has to laugh to see himself turned into a tortoise relieve the crescendo of horror in which the tale culminates. Lucius declared at the end that the story was a charming one and had made a long, uphill journey short and easy for man and beast.

The second story, Thelyphron and the Witches,[5] is also concerned with magic and laid in Thessaly, land of marvels. It is told at a dinner party given by the elegant matron Byrrhaena at her request by one of her guests, Thelyphron, to entertain the guest of honor, Lucius. Horror is the predominating note as in the story of Socrates yet the tale is preceded and followed by unrestrained laughter on the part of all the guests at the cruel joke which the witches played.

[5] *Met.* II. 20–31.

Thelyphron began his story with a simple natural account of his arrival in the market-place of Larissa and his surprise at hearing an old man proclaiming in a loud voice if anyone was willing to guard a corpse, he would be well paid. When Thelyphron inquired lightly of the old man whether here the dead were wont to run away, the reply started the gruesomeness of the tale : "Hush ! You are certainly a child and a stranger, so you don't know that you are in Thessaly where witch-women bite off bits of the faces of the dead, and use them in their magic arts."

Nothing daunted and needing money, Thelyphron took on the job of keeping the body intact, was escorted to the house of one of the chief men of the city, led into a darkened chamber and there stood beside the dead youth while in the presence of seven witnesses his mourning wife had an inventory taken of his features. Then he was left alone with a little oil lamp and the body.

First Thelyphron sang to keep awake. Then as it grew darker and darker, somehow he began to be afraid. Suddenly at midnight he saw a little weasel creep into the chamber and take its stand in front of him with a piercing look. Though he drove it out, at once he fell into so deep a slumber that he seemed another corpse, and he slept till cockcrow. In great terror on awakening he ran to the corpse with the light, uncovered the face, looked at every feature and found all sound. Then the weeping wife burst in, kissed her dead, scanned the face of her husband and finding every part safe, thanked the youth and gave him his pay. Thelyphron in his joy made a most unfortunate remark to the lady : "Madam, as often as you need my services, command me." Whereat he was man-handled by her servants and driven out of the house in dreadful state.

A little later he encountered on the street the funeral

procession of the young man and saw an amazing episode. A venerable old gentleman halted the bier and amidst his sobs proclaimed to the citizens that this his noble nephew had been murdered by his wicked wife for the sake of her lover and her inheritance.   To prove his words to the excited crowd he begged that an Egyptian priest Zatchlas should be allowed to bring back the spirit of the dead for a short time and question him.   In silent and awful rites Zatchlas performed his task.   The corpse sat up on his bier and testified : "I was poisoned by the wicked arts of my bride and gave over my bed still warm to her adulterer."   The bold woman then proceeded to wrangle with the corpse about his mendacity until he said with a groan that he could prove his truthfulness by telling them what no one else knew and pointing at Thelyphron he declared that during the watching of his body, the witches had cast sleep upon the guard, had then called the dead by name intending to mutilate him, but as Thelyphron had the same name, he got up in his sleep, walked to them and suffered the mutilation planned for the corpse ; the proof of this was the wax ears and nose that they substituted for his real ones.

When Thelyphron in horror fingered his ears and nose, all came off.   "So now," he ended, "I wear my hair long and this linen mask."   At this conclusion great laughter again burst forth.   The striking elements in this narrative are the simplicity and rapidity of the story, the naturalness of the conversations, the unexpected turns in the raising of the dead, the denunciation of the wife, the discovery of the wax features, and the cumulative horror from the dark room of the corpse, from Egyptian rites, and black magic, finally from the cruel laughter of the guests at the joke on Thelyphron.

The third story, the battle of the wineskins, has already

been described.[6] It is related by Lucius as a personal adventure which befell him at the Festival of Risus. In type it is linked with the *controversiae* of the schools because of the court-room speeches of the accuser and the accused. Events move rapidly from Lucius' slaughter of three in the dark when he was drunk, to his arrest, his trial and his final discovery that he had gashed not stalwart robbers but inflated wineskins. Inextinguishable laughter accompanies the mock trial to the discomfiture of the hero. His self-respect is eventually somewhat restored when Fotis assures him that the wineskins when he fought them, were actually living forms, animated by magic. This ending connects the story with the preceding tales of magic and prepares the way for the hero's fatal experiment in the use of magic himself.

The transformation of the hero is told in pithy, rapid narrative.[7] The witch's maid, Fotis, now completely enamored of Lucius, at dead of night secreted him in an upper bedroom where through a crack in the door he could watch Pamphile become a bird. The process was simple. Pamphile stripped, rubbed herself from tips of nails to ends of hairs with an unguent from a small box, murmured over a lamp, shook her limbs, feathered out and flew off, an owl. Now Lucius must try the rites himself. So with more lively blandishments of Fotis and fond protestations of sure return to her, he secured from her a box of the salve, rubbed well his naked body, waved his arms as though they were wings. But no plumes appeared. Hair stiffened, skin hardened to hide, fingers and toes united into hooves, from end of spine grew forth great tail ; face, mouth, nose, lips and ears grew huge. At last Lucius saw that he had become not bird, but ass ! Yet though a perfect ass he retained the mind of a man. Now

---

[6] *Met.* II. 32–III. 18, see pp. 148–49.   [7] *Met.* III. 21–25.

the worst of it was that Fotis had gathered no roses that day, for a meal of roses is the antidote for this strange change, so Lucius must wait in stable with his own horse and another ass until in morning light Fotis could secure the remedy. But during the night thieves robbed the house and stole Lucius to carry off their pelf. Long months passed before he munched the rose-petals and became himself again.

Hereon Lucius, the man-ass, becomes the narrator of the novel, and this four-footed human, with his keen understanding of both men and beasts, is the bizarre interpreter of the pageant of life which advances before us. The robbers now took him to their mountain refuge and there he observed their life and heard their exploits told.

The next three stories, 4, 5, 6, form a group of tales about the chieftains of these robbers.[8] They are stories of adventure told at dinner in the robbers' cave by one of the band to the others. A description of their mountain stronghold gives a realistic and romantic setting for the stories. The first two are very short and rapid, but none the less effective.

The scene of the first, the story of Lamachus, is in Thebes, the house of a rich miser, Chryseros, which the band of thieves plans to rob. In the darkness of night the robbers crept up outside to the door but inside Chryseros had heard them and was creeping toward it too. So when the gallant Lamachus put his hand through the great key-hole to pull back the bar Chryseros was ready and suddenly drove a huge nail through the robber's hand, fastening it to the wood of the door. Then he went to the roof and with great cunning shouted to his neighbors that his house was on fire, knowing they would bring aid to protect their own. The robbers in order not to be

[8] *Met.* IV. 6–22.

caught and not to desert their companion with his consent chopped off his arm near the shoulder and hastily bandaging the stump carried off the rest of Lamachus. It was clear that his condition would keep their flight from being successful. So when his prayers to be slain had no avail, though he declared that a brave robber could not live without his right hand, with his left hand he drew his sword, kissed it and with one strong blow drove it through his heart. The robbers committed the body of their great-souled hero to the sea.

Lamachus was a gallant captain who met his end in a way worthy of his valor. But the story of Alcimus is a sordid tale of petty robbery and silly deception. Alcimus broke into the hut of a poor old woman who was asleep, went upstairs to her bedroom, tossed all her little possessions out of the window and even rolled her out of her bed to get the blankets. Of course he ought to have strangled her first. The cunning old hag fell at his feet and begged him not to throw her pitiful little rags out to her rich neighbors whose grounds her window overlooked. Alcimus deceived by her plausibility ran at once to the window and leaned far out to see if she were telling the truth when the old baggage gave him a sudden shove from behind that threw him out in the air. The fall from the high window on a great rock crushed his body, streams of blood gushed from his mouth, and after telling what had happened he gave up the ghost. So he followed Lamachus as his squire.

The third story, the tale of Thrasyleon and the bears, is much longer and has more of a plot. The scene is Plataea. The thieves planned to rob the house of a rich generous magnate, Demochares, who gave games to amuse the people. He had planned an exhibition of bears but unfortunately the beasts were dying in captivity and their

great carcasses might be seen in the streets, thrown out
for the people to use.   The robbers devised and carried
out a plan of skinning one of these, curing the hide, dress-
ing one of their number in it, and then presenting him in
a cage to Demochares.   Once inside the house he could
open it at night to his comrades.   Thrasyllus claimed the
honor of the daring adventure.   All went as planned until
as he was stealing from his cage to the door at dead of
night, a young servant saw the bear loose and gave an
alarm.   All the servants gathered with torches and lan-
terns, with clubs and lances.   All the hunting dogs were
let loose.   Of course there was no hope for Thrasyllus in
his fight, but to the end he never betrayed his comrades :
even his cries as he died imitated the howls of a beast.
Not till noon the next day did anyone learn that he was
not a bear but a man.   So he won great glory.

At the end of the three tales the robbers poured libation
of pure wine from golden goblets to the memory of their
lost companions and sang hymns to Mars before they went
to rest, a fitting ending to these dashing, rapid narratives
of adventure.

The success of the stories is due largely to the portrayal
of the psychology of the robbers which is shown in part by
having one of the band relate the tales with comments on
the little mistakes and the great heroism of their chieftains.

The story that follows is of an entirely different type
from the preceding stories of magic and adventure.   It is
a tragic romance of a kidnaped bride, Charite.[9]   It is a
very long story in three parts and it includes another long
story, the loves of Cupid and Psyche.[10]   These two stories
together form the central heart of the novel in position,
theme and significance.   Their importance demands
careful analysis.

[9] *Met*. IV. 23–27 ; VI. 25–VII. 14 ; VIII. 1–15.   [10] *Met*. IV. 28–VI. 24.

The first two parts of the story are set in the robbers' cave and are told by Lucius the Ass. Part one describes the return of the robbers to their cave with the kidnaped bride, their assurance to her that she will not be harmed, but only held until her family pays a ransom, the girl's wild grief and her narrative to the old hag of how she had been kidnaped on her wedding night, her dreadful dream of her husband's death and finally the old woman's offer to divert her by telling her some charming old wives' tale. So at the robbers' cave the old dame related to Charite the love-story of Cupid and Psyche.

After this long narrative, in part two, Charite and the ass attempted to escape but were recaptured by the robbers. The old woman meanwhile had hanged herself in fright over the loss of her charge. The robbers made awful plans for punishing Charite and the ass, but in the midst of them a new robber, Haemus, arrived who proved so gallant from his own autobiography that he was declared their new leader. Having now their confidence, he got them all drunk, revealed himself as the disguised husband of Charite, carried her home on the ass's back, then returned with helpers and dispatched her drunken captors. Here ended part two.

Lucius the Ass who was supposed to be rewarded by being turned loose in happy pasturage had by evil chance more wretched adventures until in a neighboring village he finally heard the end of the story of Charite. Part three was told by a servant of her family by the fireside at nightfall to a company of ostlers, shepherds and cowherds.

Charite was living happily with her husband, Tlepolemus, when a former suitor of hers, Thrasyllus, began to play the villain. Feigning friendship to her husband, he persuaded him to go off hunting. In the wood he had a wild boar introduced among the harmless game and while

Tlepolemus was valiantly attacking it, he secretly murdered him. The grief of Charite knew no bounds. And when Thrasyllus soon declared his passion and proposed marriage, she was overcome with horror and put off his suit.

Meanwhile the ghost of Tlepolemus appeared to her and bade her if her memory of him had faded, to marry anyone else rather than his enemy Thrasyllus, for his hands were stained with her husband's blood. Charite aghast at the truth developed a subtle plan for vengeance. She seemed gradually to yield to Thrasyllus' importunities, but told him that she must wait the conventional year of mourning before marrying him ; however, she would grant him his desire if he would come secretly to her bedroom ; there her old nurse would admit him. That very night Thrasyllus arrived, was let in, was told by the nurse that Charite was delayed by attendance on her ill father, and was given drugged wine which plunged him into deep slumber.

Then over his prostrate body Charite pronounced her curse and his doom and after her speech, with a great pin from her hair she stabbed out his eyes. Then she fled to her husband's sepulchre. Those who saw her running followed her, but could not halt her deed, for she brandished a sword wildly and keeping them at a distance told them of the vengeance she had taken, then stabbed herself over Tlepolemus' tomb. When Thrasyllus learned her fate, he felt that death on his sword could not atone for the ruin he had caused, so he had himself shut up in the sepulchre of the unhappy pair and there met death by starvation. All the rustics wept as they heard the end of this tragic romance.

The technique of this narrative is consummate. Scenes shift quickly before our eyes : Charite's home on the wedding night, the robbers' mountain cave, the forest where the men go hunting, the bedroom of Charite where she blinds her wicked lover, her husband's sepulchre. The telling is varied by the ass's comments, the old hag's fairy-story of Cupid and Psyche, Charite's dream of her husband, the apparition of his ghost. The element of the horrible is not lacking because of the awful punishment planned by the thieves for Charite and the ass after their attempted escape, the pitiful body of the old hag hanging from a tree, Charite's blinding of her false lover.

Conversation and speeches are used constantly to enliven narration, some of them as dramatic as the messenger's speech in tragedy in narrating past events, some revealing character, some surcharged with feeling. The element of suspense is used with great effect through the break in the narrative for the telling of the story of Cupid and Psyche, and the interest is heightened by the unexpected reversal of fortune that turned romance into tragedy, and by the surprise in the repentance of the villain at the end, so that by his voluntary death he too is clothed in a certain nobility. The whole story is pregnant with emotion all centering in the story of Charite and her love for her husband. This novelette within Apuleius' great novel is the best developed tragic romance in Latin literature.

The story of Cupid and Psyche is another tale of a kidnaped bride included in Charite's story as a kind of divine counterpart to her earthly sufferings to assure her of a happy issue out of all her misfortunes. In origin it is a fairy-story and this folk-lore element is suggested by the fact that the old crone who relates it says she is going to tell an old wives' tale. Moreover it is lifted at once out of reality to the sky because the lovers are given symbolic names Cupid, Love, Psyche, the Soul, and are surrounded by the great hierarchy of Olympian gods. Cupid's jealous, cruel mother is Venus herself. Cupid's father who finally bestows happiness upon him in the girl of his choice is Jupiter, king of the gods.

Of so long a story only a brief outline can be given. A mortal maid, Psyche, was so worshiped for her great beauty that Venus' shrines were deserted. Venus outraged at this insult pointed her out to her son Cupid and ordered him to take vengeance on the girl by making her fall in love with some mean churl whom she must wed. Now the girl since she was regarded as a goddess had no suitors though her two sisters were easily married. Her father on consulting the oracle of Apollo was told that his daughter must be left alone on the top of a high mountain to be the bride of a serpent. The procession to the hill-top had more of funeral pomp than wedding joy. But left alone Psyche was gently carried off by the wind Zephyrus to a marvelous palace where unseen servants waited on her ; unseen musicians played to her ; and in the dark an unseen lover made her his own.

The conditions of her happy union were simple : never to see her husband's face, never to see her sisters for fear of sure disaster. But the simple Psyche lonely all the day finally persuaded her lover to let Zephyr bring her sisters to the palace. Her wealth aroused their jealousy. Her palpable deception about her husband convinced them that she did not know who he was. So in their third visit the wicked sisters in spite of all Cupid's warnings were able to persuade Psyche that the serpent of the oracle was sleeping with her ; and that she must hide lamp and razor by the bed and at last discover and slay the monster.

The light revealed no dragon but a fair young god who

now awakening told Psyche that they were betrayed to woe and flew off. Then comes the tale of Psyche's sufferings. She attempted self-destruction in a river, but the river refused to drown Love's Lady. The great god Pan tried to give her cheer and courage. Already Venus had heard from a gossip gull that her son was enamored of her rival and in rage upbraided him and confided her indignation to Juno and Ceres. So when Psyche appealed to each of these goddesses, neither dared aid her.

Venus now through the aid of Jupiter and Mercury claimed Psyche as a runaway slave, got possession of her and set her cruel tasks. But nature rose to aid the Love of Love, so Psyche sorted the pile of grain by the help of nimble ants, secured a flock of golden fleece by the advice of a talking reed, received jar of water of the Styx from eagle's talons, and a box of Proserpina's beauty by the counsel of the tower that talked.

In the last task Psyche's besetting sin of curiosity almost destroyed her, for she opened the box to secure if she could more beauty for herself. Then a deadly slumber fell upon her and she might have been lost in it had not Cupid himself roused her. Thus at last her lover became her savior, for he flew on high to Jupiter and won his father's consent to marriage with his love. In council of the Olympians, Jupiter himself decreed that Venus should lay aside her enmity, that Mercury should bring the mortal girl to heaven to be made immortal and that there among the gods there should be celebrated the royal marriage of Cupid and Psyche. In due time from that union was born Joy.

The barest outline of this famous story shows the interweaving of different colored threads in its pattern. Folklore contributed the main elements of the story itself (unhappy girl, jealous sisters, invisible husband, cruel step-mother) and the miraculous element of talking birds, ants, beasts, reed, tower. The Olympian religion lifted the old wives' tale to a glamorous setting of divine splendor. A faint echo of Platonism gave symbolic names to the lovers, to their child, to the servants of Venus. And the Milesian tales as Apuleius himself acknowledged lent romance to this sublimated form of their well-known type of story. But out of all these familiar elements Apuleius created a new fabric of great originality and beauty.

The pictorial character of the narrative is at first the most striking. Scene after scene is impressed on memory with an almost tangible visibility : fair young Psyche walking through adoring crowds ; Zephyr wafting the sleeping beauty through the air ; Cupid's gleaming palace ; the discovery of the sleeping God of Love by the lamp's light ; the irate Venus talking to her peers ; Psyche tortured by Venus' servants ; Psyche before Proserpina in Hades ; Cupid before Jupiter ; the Council of the Gods ; the Wedding Banquet. No wonder that after Raphael discovered the value for painting of these word-pictures the Renaissance went mad over the scenes so that artists used them in Castel of S. Angelo for a Pope, in Palazzo del Tè for the d'Estes of Mantua, and European painters and sculptors down to the present have kept repeating the themes. Apuleius himself by the realistic details of his descriptions and the suggested effects still stimulates the imagination to re-creation.

His palette was set with words and nowhere else in his novel is there such an elaborate use of sound for musical effects as in this story. A rich diction composed of archaisms and of current coinage is arranged in rhythmic and rhymed phrases in cunning antitheses, with key-note repetitions of words and letters until a melody is produced

that carries the beauty of the tale itself to sweeter meaning. No translation can reproduce this melodic Latin :
it must be *heard* in all its own singing quality.

Much conversation varies the *purpurei panni* of descriptions and enlivens the steady flow of the narrative.
Not only mortals and gods hold converse, but gull chatters,
ants utter wise reflections, reed and tower give advice,
lethal waters proclaim warnings, even lamp and razor express without words their feelings. The whole world is
sentient and surrounds Psyche with sympathy of word,
music or action. Finally at her wedding even the Hours
come flower-laden, the Graces scatter balsam, and the
Muses sing her marriage hymn. Never was there a more
glamorous or more sensuous story.

The story of Cupid and Psyche was related as an inset
in the tragic romance of Charite. After that sorrowful
tale of true love was finished, the ass's adventures continued and included a period with a corrupt band of lewd
Syrian priests. The next major stories are four Milesian
tales which have none of the sublimated character of the
Psyche story, but are full of the original naughtiness and
frivolity of the type. One stands alone ; the other three
are interlaced in one group.

The story of the Lover under the Tub is told by Lucius
the ass to the readers of the novel. It happened in a
certain rich city. The characters are a poor blacksmith,
his wanton wife and her *amante*. When her husband
went out to work one morning, in came her lover. But
that day the smith returned home very early, and whistled
outside the door to his wife to let him in, being much
pleased that his chaste spouse had the doors fast locked.
At the whistle, the resourceful woman hid her lover under
a large tub, then let her husband in with much vitupera-
tion because he had not worked long enough to earn a

day's food for them.   Her husband protested that she was
mistaken for he had been out selling their old tub for
five *denarii* and must at once clean it for the purchaser,
who would soon arrive.   Quick as a wink his wife retorted that she had already sold it for seven *denarii* and
her purchaser was even now under the tub, investigating
its solidity.   Her lover shouted out confirmation of her
words.   At this the husband begged the purchaser to
come out and let him himself clean the tub for him.   So
out came lover, in went husband.   And on the top of
the tub wife and lover made love while husband worked
inside.   The deceived smith finally even had to carry the
tub on his back to the home of the adulterer !   Two and
a half pages full of conversation relate the story of the
simple blacksmith and his lively wanton, *lepidam de
adulterio cuiusdam pauperis fabulam*.[11]

The story of the baker's wife is much longer and more
elaborate.[12]   It too is related by Lucius the ass.   Within
it are included two other stories of adultery, one told by
a bawd, the other by the deceived baker.   The irony of
the whole tale is intensified by the fact that the ass, Lucius,
is the narrator and his standards of morality are outraged
by the wickedness of the women.   The ass begins with
a long vituperative character sketch of the baker's wife
into whose soul all crime had flowed as into a filthy privy,
and describes his sympathy for her honest husband's lot
and his own beatings and hard labor under her cruelty.
The ass then introduces the other characters in the story,
young lover, corrupting procuress, and to show the character of the old bawd, he relates a story she told the baker's
wife to persuade her to change a dull lover for Philesitherus.   The ass suggests his horrified relish of the story

[11] *Met.* IX. 5–7.   [12] *Met.* IX. 11–31.

stating that one comfort he had in this transformation to an ass was that his long ears could hear everything.

The bawd's story of the Sandals under the Bed has four characters, Barbarus, the husband, his beautiful wife, Arete, her lover, Philesitherus, and Barbarus' slave, Myrmex. The central event is the unexpected return of the husband from his travels.

When Barbarus went off on a journey, he secretly ordered his slave to guard his beautiful wife, never leaving her if he valued his own life. In spite of such precautions her great beauty caught the eye of Philesitherus, who decided that the only way to get her was through the slave. Believing that all human nature is frail and that gold can break through doors of adamant, Philesitherus found Myrmex alone, told his love, showed him thirty pieces of gold and told him twenty would go to the Lady and ten to Myrmex if his suit was successful. A frightful struggle went on in Myrmex's mind between fear of punishment from his master and desire for the gold pieces. Finally he resolved to let his mistress make her own decision. She did not hesitate a moment to accept Philesitherus' offer. So that night Myrmex brought the lover, all muffled up, to his Lady's room. But about midnight Barbarus, unexpectedly returning, knocked on the door, shouted, threw stones at it, becoming more and more suspicious with the long delay. When Philesitherus got out of the chamber, Myrmex, who had pretended that he could not find the key, admitted Barbarus. While he rushed to his wife's room, Myrmex let the lover out by a side door.

In the morning, Barbarus saw a pair of strange sandals under his bed. Aghast at their significance, he said nothing, hid them in his robe, had Myrmex bound and started off with the groaning slave to the forum, sure that he could find the adulterer by the evidence of the sandals. Philesitherus happening to meet them, took in the situation at a glance, remembering what he had left behind him. So with quick ingenuity he rushed at Myrmex, belabored him and demanded back his sandals which he declared Myrmex had stolen from him at the baths the night before. Barbarus, completely convinced by Philesitherus' quick plausibility, returned home at once, pardoned Myrmex and gave him the sandals to deliver to their lawful owner !

The story was told by the bawd to show the type of valiant, ingenious lover that the baker's wife should look for instead of the puling, timid youth who enjoyed her favors. The story had its effect and the bawd returned that evening with Philesitherus, the new lover, who was made most welcome at a fine supper while the ass looked on. But hardly had the youth begun to eat or drink, when the husband came home early. The baker's wife quickly hid her lover under a wooden bin in which she was wont to sift grain. Then with an expression of innocent surprise she asked her husband why he had left the dinner-party of his friend, the fuller, so early.

The husband, full of horror at what had happened at the dinner, explained by relating the story of the fuller's wife. This woman who had always been supposed a model of virtue had secretly taken a lover. That very night they were together when her husband and the baker came in from the baths to dinner. The woman hid her friend in a sulphur-vat over which clothes were hung to be cleaned, and feeling quite secure took her place at the table. But suddenly the youth began to sneeze from the sulphur fumes and was discovered by the husband, who demanded a sword to kill him. The baker after persuading his friend to carry the youth out and leave him to die from choking caused by the sulphur, and the wife to go to a friend's house until her husband's anger passed, had come home in disgust.

The baker's wife was loud in her denunciation of the corruption of the fuller's wife. This was more than the virtuous ass could bear and when chance enabled him to reveal the character of the woman, he seized it. As he was being led out to be watered, he saw the lover's fingers projecting from under the bin and trod upon them so that the young man screamed and was discovered. The husband took an ironic vengeance by using the boy for his own lust ; then had him beaten and driven out by his slaves, and finally divorced his wife. That terrible female, though conscious of receiving her deserts, at once plotted vengeance, securing the help of an old witch. One day the ass saw a pitiful woman come into the mill, all ragged, thin, unkempt, with ashes on her head. She took the baker by the hand and led him into a room as if she had something to confide to him. The door was shut behind them. When all the grain was ground, the slaves called their master to give them more work. No answer came to their shouts or their knocking. When they broke down the door, there was no woman in the room, but their master was hanging from a beam, dead. The next day the baker's daughter who lived with her husband in a nearby village arrived in mourning because an apparition of her father with a rope about his neck appearing in the night had told her all the story of her step-mother, her adultery, her witchcraft, and his death.

This is a very elaborate, carefully constructed story of adultery, varied by two inserted tales of woman's faithlessness, and related with much irony by the ass, whose keen observation and outraged sensibilities add poignancy to the pictures of woman's frailty. Long descriptions, caustic comments, conversation, stories within stories diversify the art of narration. The group illustrates Apuleius' most elaborate use of the original type of Milesian tale.

The next story [13] from its theme of the struggle of the poor against the rich recalls the fictitious cases of the rhetorical schools in the *controversiae* of Seneca. It is told by Lucius the Ass with his usual sympathy for the poor and oppressed. The ass's master was now a gardener who poor though he was could offer shelter and hospitality to a belated traveler on a dark, rainy night. The traveler to reward his poor host promised him a gift of grain, oil and wine if he would ride to his house next day. So master and ass journeyed there, but while the gardener was enjoying dinner with his new friend, terrible events occurred. There were warnings of them, for hideous omens appeared, one a miraculous fountain of blood which suddenly besprinkled the table. Presently a slave bursting in related the awful disaster which had befallen the house.

The host had three fine sons, well educated, virtuous. They were friends of a poor neighbor who was being constantly oppressed by a rich young noble whose lands joined his. The rich man had killed the poor man's sheep, stolen his oxen, destroyed his crops and finally on some trumped-up dispute over boundaries had claimed all his farm. The poor man wishing to save at least enough of his father's land to be buried in had summoned all his neighbors, among them the three brothers, for a demonstration of protest to the rich noble. When mild statements had no effect, one of the three brothers, said boldly that it was futile for the noble trusting in his wealth

13 *Met.* IX. 33–38.

to threaten tyrannical acts, for there were laws that protected the poor from the insolence of the rich.

The young noble was so incensed by this speech, that
he had his fierce mastiffs loosed by his shepherds and
ordered to attack the company. The fight was horrible
and there was no escape. The youngest of the three
brothers as he tried to run away, tripped, fell, and was
torn to pieces by the dogs. As the other two sought to
aid their brother, a second was transfixed by a lance hurled
by the rich man. The lance was thrown with such force
that after it pierced the body the point was buried in
the ground and the lance held the youth upright as he
died, swaying on the weapon. The third brother by his
cunning was able to kill the tyrant in vengeance and
before the servants could fall upon him, he stabbed his
own throat with the knife wet with his enemy's blood.

When the father heard all the tale of the death of his
three sons, he could not say a word or shed a tear. He
simply seized the knife with which he had just cut up
cheese and food for his guests and stabbed his own throat
as his most unhappy son had done. And as he fell forward on the table, his gushing blood wiped out the stains
of the miraculous drops of the awful omen.

The story is a very short one but it is full of horror
produced by realistic details, increased by the sympathy
of Lucius for the oppression of the poor, and emphasized
by the two brief speeches of one of the three gallant
brothers.

Story XIV, the amorous stepmother,[14] is a tale of
such a horrible crime that Lucius thinks it should be
recorded. The main interest is in the plot ; the setting
is not localized ; the characters are not even named but
are stock characters like those of the new comedy ; and

[14] *Met.* X. 2–12.

the development of the action is brought about chiefly through long speeches, savoring of the rhetoric of the schools.   The fact that the ironic ass is the narrator of the tale and that Apuleius himself once breaks through that long-eared disguise to address his Excellent Reader diversify the method of telling the story.

In a certain little state a terrible crime was committed. It happened in a family composed of four persons : a centurion, master of the house, his son by his first wife, a young man of fine education and excellent character, the second wife, noted more for beauty than for virtue, a little boy, twelve years old, son of the head of the house and of his second wife.   The beginning of all the trouble was that the stepmother fell in love with her stepson. "Now," says Apuleius, "know, Noble Reader, that you are going to hear a tragedy, not a little story, and you are leaving sock for buskin."

The stepmother at first struggled with her passion and concealed it so that all, even the learned doctors, thought she was very ill, but anyone versed in love's madness could have diagnosed her state.   At last overcome she sent for her stepson and offered herself to him in a specious plea : "You are the cause of my sickness ; you alone can be its cure.   Your eyes have set me on fire.   Pity one who is dying for you.   Let not loyalty to your sire restrain you. You will save for him his wife.   It is his likeness in you that I love.   Opportunity is easy.   What no one knows is hardly done."

The stepson though surprised and horrified showed great wisdom on seeing her plight, spoke gently to her, made promises about the future, begged her to restore her health and urged her to wait until his father was away. Thus escaping he at once sought advice from his wise old tutor, who urged him to fly.   But before he could

start, the stepmother got her husband off on a long journey and demanded the fulfilment of her stepson's promises.   When he put her off by one excuse after another,
she discerned his real feeling.   Her love turned to hate
and she decided with the help of a wicked slave to take
vengeance.   A cup of poisoned wine was now prepared
for her stepson, but her little boy, coming home from
school at noon, being thirsty after his lunch, found the
wine, drank it and fell to the ground lifeless.   Even by
this catastrophe the mother's mind was not diverted from
revenge.   Sending for her husband, she told him that
the boy had been killed by his brother's poison ; that his
brother had tried to force her love and when unsuccessful
had threatened her with a sword if she divulged his advances.

So the grief-stricken father saw that he must lose two
sons at once, and after the funeral of the boy he had to
accuse his older son of murder.   Senate and people were
so filled with horror at his deeds that they demanded that
he be stoned to death without a trial, but the magistrates
implored them to follow the customs of their ancestors, to
condemn no one unheard, to examine witnesses on both
sides, to have a trial and a sentence as civilized nations
were accustomed to do in times of peace.   Their appeal
prevailed, and the case was presented with proper speeches
and witnesses.   (Here the ass omits much of the tedious
procedure of the court-room, giving as an ironical excuse
that he could not hear it, for he was in his stable !)   Finally the wicked slave was produced and gave false witness that the young man had tried to get his aid in taking
vengeance on his stepmother for her rejection of him and
failing in that had poisoned the boy himself.

At this the case seemed concluded and all the judges
were about to write "guilty" on their votes when one of

the oldest of the senators, a distinguished physician, arose. He revealed that the slave had come to him to purchase a quick poison for a dying man ; that he had made the slave seal with his own seal the bag of gold paid as his fee, now produced in court as evidence ; and that finally, suspecting mischief, he had sold not a poison but a powerful sleeping draught, so that if his story were true, the boy would be found not dead but sleeping.   At the conclusion of this speech the whole court and indeed all the town people rushed to the tomb where the child lay. The father himself opened the coffin and found his little son shaking off the effects of the potion and ready to embrace him.   Just as he was, in his shroud, he was shown to the people and carried to the court-room.   There sentence of eternal exile was pronounced on the woman. The slave was condemned to the gallows.   The physician was told to keep the gold.   The aged father found that both his sons were restored to him.

The rapidity of the narrative prevents interest from flagging though the story is the familiar Phaedra type. The addition of the cup of poison and the supposed death of the little boy vary the plot.   The thoroughly Roman trial scene, the amazing resurrection at the tomb set off each other by contrast.   The ass as narrator with his touches of irony about legal procedure and physicians' diagnoses adds a bizarre element.   The most notable feature of the story is the use of speeches to develop the plot, especially the two long, rhetorical speeches of the courtroom.   A simple *novella* has become, under the influence of tragedy, new comedy, and the rhetorical schools, this elaborate tale.

The last major story introduced into the plot, XV, is that of the Murderess of Five.[15]   The ass relates with

15 *Met.* X. 23–28.

horror the story of a criminal woman, who was condemned to be eaten by wild beasts, and who is to be shown to the public with the ass in obscene exhibition in the theater. The first murder that the woman committed was of her husband's sister. This girl had been reared secretly by her own mother against her husband's express orders that any girl baby born in his absence should be killed. Her brother, in whom their mother had confided, was giving her the hospitality of his home, pretending that she was the daughter of a neighbor who had lost both parents and fortune. The brother's wife, not knowing who she was, was jealous of her and to get rid of her stole her husband's signet ring, and sent it to her with a message that she should come at once to the country to the owner of the ring. The girl was trapped, beaten cruelly and, although she declared her true relationship to her brother, she was murdered by being impaled on a burning fagot.

When her brother learned the horror of this awful murder, he fell into a raving fever. His wife to finish him too negotiated with a certain physician at the price of fifty gold pieces for a deadly poison. When the physician brought the potion, she told her husband and his assembled relatives that she had ordered a medicinal draught for the sick man's recovery, and to reassure them she would ask the physician to drink part of it before them all. (She did this to rid herself of the only witness against her and to save the gold she had promised the doctor !) The physician completely caught had to drink a good part of the poison and was unable to rush home and take an antidote because the wicked woman detained him until she saw the draught was beginning to work. He had hardly told his wife the whole story and bequeathed her the collection of his fee when he died. The young husband also passed away.

The physician's wife a few days afterwards went and demanded her husband's fee. The murderess assured her she would give her the whole amount if she would only bring her a little more of the poison. This the physician's wife stupidly did. Now the murderess decided to get rid of her young daughter who was her father's heir so that she herself could succeed to the property. And to make two hits with one stone, she invited the physician's wife to dinner and poisoned her and the child at the same meal. The child, being young and delicate, died at once. The physician's wife lived long enough to get to the judge's house, and reveal the whole series of crimes before she expired. The murderess was condemned to be thrown to wild beasts.

This is a straightforward plain narrative of the crimes of an ingenious sadist. Horror is the chief emotion produced by the story, but cruelty, jealousy, cupidity, and cunning have their share in the action.

Besides these fifteen tales which I have called major stories there are many incidental stories which advance the plot by enlivening its progress or diversifying the interests involved. Some are mere parts of the narrative. Some are little character sketches. Some add atmosphere to a particular scene. Some by contrast present foils to more important characters or episodes.

To illustrate, between the first two stories both about magic three character sketches are introduced. The first is a miniature of the officious aedile Pythias [16] whose pompous inefficiency is portrayed in lively conversation. The second is a long realistic description of the maid Fotis [17] whose presence is essential to the development of the plot because she enables Lucius to see and copy the magic arts of her witch mistress. Her wanton character

[16] *Met.* I. 24–25.　　　　[17] *Met.* II. 6–17, III. 13–26.

also prepares the way for the salaciousness of the Milesian Tales. The third sketch is of the foolish Assyrian sooth-sayer, Diophanes,[18] who loses the fee of a good client by stupidly relating in his presence how little his prophetic powers helped himself in his travels. Taken out of his place in the narrative, he makes a companion piece to the powerful Egyptian prophet, Zatchlas, who was able to raise the dead in order to convict a murderess.[19]

An incidental story of robbers is the short narrative of his own prowess related in the robbers' cave by Tlepole-mus, when he is posing as the famous bandit Haemus.[20] This is introduced to develop the plot and win the robbers by a tale after their own hearts to accept Haemus as a new leader. They do not perceive the ironic humor with which Haemus relates how the virtuous Plotina, mother of ten, devoted wife of an official in the court of the emperor, caused the downfall of Haemus' former band or how drily his story hints that Charite will wreak vengeance on her captors.

Incidental stories which give atmosphere and back-ground are tales which show the hard lives of shepherds and their beasts. Such are the anecdote of the great bear and the bad boy,[21] the fight of the innocent shepherds with the suspicious villagers,[22] the mysterious death of a young shepherd in a dragon's cave,[23] the torture of a slave by ants,[24] the overbearing soldier who robbed a gardener of the ass.[25] Brief as several of these are (a single page in the Teubner text) they are effective in their vividness for enriching the novel by multiplying types of characters, by intensifying atmosphere or by emphasizing the op-pression and the sufferings of the poor.

---

[18] *Met.* II. 12–14. [19] *Met.* II. 28–30. [20] *Met.* VI. 4–9.
[21] *Met.* VII. 24–28. [22] *Met.* VIII. 15–18. [23] *Met.* VIII. 19–21.
[24] *Met.* VIII. 22. [25] *Met.* IX. 39–42.

The most amazing part of this multicolored novel is the eleventh book.   This is the account of the restoration of Lucius to human form through the beneficence of the goddess Isis.   Here Apuleius breaks away from the plot of his Greek original and from the Milesian tales which he interwove into so rich a tapestry.   Here are no *novelle*.   The book is a sober narrative of a great religious experience.   The conversion of Lucius is related in solemn language with mystic symbolism.   Lucius is identified with "a poor man of Madaura," that is, Apuleius himself, and the Reader is conducted into intimate observation of the rites of Isis.   The religious fervor manifested in the cult makes the greatest contrast with the last story of Book X (The Murderess of Five) and the plans for the obscene exhibition in which Lucius was to be displayed with the murderess.

Now in this account of a religious experience the narrative art of Apuleius is displayed no less than in his short stories.   An analysis of the book will show the varied devices by which he leads the reader to an emotional receptivity for the tale of his initiation.   Lucius the ass having escaped from the spectacle at Corinth found himself on the shore of Cenchreae and there close by the sea he slept.   Startled out of slumber by the light of the full moon as it rose from the sea, Lucius thought of that goddess of light who informs and illuminates all the world and with sudden hope of safety offered to her impassioned prayer for deliverance.   Again he slept and now a vision appeared before him of the goddess herself rising bright and luminous from mid-ocean in mystic robe, and at last she deigned to speak to him, revealing herself.   Salvation is what she promises him, for at her spring festival of the launching of the ship her priest will give him the meal of roses and he will lose the hide and form of ass which she abhors. In return all the rest of his life must be dedicated to the goddess who is his savior and after death he will see her again face to face and adore her.

Lucius awoke in rapture to a bright spring day of singing birds, budding trees, gentle zephyrs, and found that on that very day the ceremony of the launching of the ship was to occur. All Apuleius' powers of description color the pageantry of that great pomp. And against so brilliant a scene Lucius was given the roses and became a man again, a miracle that increased the joy of all the votaries of Isis. The priest who conferred the flowers in serious homily interpreted for Lucius his experiences and advised him for the future. From the sins of youth, lust and curiosity, from the blows of blind Fortune, he has come to the harbor of peace and the altar of pity ; he has been freed by the providence of great Isis ; saved by her grace he must enter her service so to enjoy the full blessing of freedom. Then the procession with Lucius among the votaries went on to the sea, the bark of Isis was launched, the *corteo* returned to the temple where the priest offered prayer for Emperor, Senate, Knights, all the Roman people, for all ships and for those in peril on the sea, and dismissed the crowd.

Lucius thereafter haunted the temple waiting for new orders. Finally the goddess appearing in another vision announced that his day of initiation was at hand and her priest Mithras would inform him about proper preparations. So after instruction from mystic books, ablutions, fasting for ten days, at last Lucius experienced the awful final rites : he died, he rose from the dead and journeyed through all the elements ; at midnight he saw the sun shining brightly, he approached the gods below and the gods above face to face and worshiped them in their presence.   After this mystic revelation, Lucius himself assumed the guise of the sun-god, stood as if divine upon a pedestal before the image of the goddess, was seen by all the people, and honored with religious feast.   Finally his ecstatic experience was ended by a devout prayer of passionate dedication addressed to his adored Lady Isis.

The tempo of the rest of the book is slower and quieter. Lucius after traveling to Rome is again admonished in sleep of the need of new initiation into the cult of Osiris and finally "the poor man of Madaura" is again initiated into the rites of the god and becomes forever a priest of the Egyptian cult.   Lucius the gay young adventurer has been completely transformed once more into this member of the College of the Pastophores with shaven head and linen stole.

A perusal of the eleventh book will convince any reader that Apuleius' finest technique is employed in the narrative.   A mystic religious experience is made real by settings of moon-lit seashore, spring day, brilliant pageantry, dark temple.   Goddess in radiant vision is depicted in detailed description.   Direct speech is used in prayers, revelations from goddess, benediction of priest. Lucius now become Apuleius relates directly to the reader all that it is lawful for the uninitiate to hear about his initiation.   Finally little by little the reader becomes aware that the hero is standing before him in new guise, a transformed soul.

This analysis of the major stories in sequence, the summary of the incidental stories, and their relation to the plot, and the analysis of Book XI has put us in a position to consider the narrative art of Apuleius in his whole novel.   First of all his *novelle* are surprisingly short.   Of the fifteen most important ones, five cover less than ten pages in the Teubner text and in the two groups of stories (the robber chiefs, the Milesian Tales) one group covers thirteen pages, the other fifteen. There are only two really long *novelle,* the story of Charite which for its three parts demanded thirty-five pages, and the story of Cupid and Psyche which included fifty-one. These *novelle* (the Charite-Psyche stories) in the center of the novel therefore overbalance in proportion the great last book of the retransformation through the worship of Isis which is described in twenty-five pages. In considering the length of the different stories it is worth noting that the salacious tales form only a small proportion of the whole novel ; also that the narrative art of Apuleius is as consummate in the two-page stories of the robber chiefs, Lamachus and Alcimus, and of the Lover under the Tub as in the long tragic romance of Charite.

Part of this art consists in the personality of the narrator and his relation to his audience. The *Metamorphoses* is an *ich-roman,* a story told by Lucius in the first person to the reader who is often directly addressed. This personal character of the narration is diversified by having several of the major stories told by some special character to a special audience. The story of Socrates and the witch is told to two fellow-travelers on the road, one of whom is Lucius, so here the chief narrator of the novel becomes audience. This is true in the story of Thelyphron and the witches, which is told by Thelyphron at a dinner-party for the benefit of the guest of honor, Lucius. The three stories of robber chiefs are told by one robber to the rest of the band at dinner in their cave while Lucius the ass listens. Lucius himself narrates the long tale of Charite but the inset, Cupid and Psyche, is told by the old crone who keeps the robbers' cave to the kidnaped bride, and the third part of Charite's story by a servant from her family. In the four Milesian tales that follow Lucius the ass recounts the stories of the Lover under the Tub and the Baker's Wife, but in the two stories included in that of the Baker's Wife an old procuress tells the story of the Sandals under the Bed to the Baker's Wife, and the Baker relates the story of the Fuller's Wife to his own spouse. Lucius the ass is the narrator of the next story about the Rich Man and the Poor Man but in it a messenger appears as in Greek tragedy to relate the awful deaths of the three sons of the poor man's neighbor. Lucius the Ass tells the tragic romance of the Amorous Stepmother and the tale of the Murderess of Five. Lucius too recounts the crucial events which motivate the entire plot, his transformation and his retransformation.

A certain subtle development in the relation of Lucius to the reader may be traced in the progress of the novel. The first chapter brings him *en rapport* with his audience. Lucius identifies himself as a Greek with progenitors of Athens, Corinth and Sparta. He states his theme, the transformations and retransformations of men and their fortunes. He states the sources of his novel : a Greek story, Milesian tales. He declares that his style is exotic and forensic, due to the fact that Latin was an acquired language. But he assures the reader that if he listens to the story, he will be entertained.

After Lucius is transformed into an ass, he often reminds the reader that though now a perfect ass he has retained human intelligence [26] and curiosity.[27] He makes moral comments on the characters in the novel, on the venality of women,[28] on the blindness of Fortune.[29] He reflects that his ass form has given him the opportunity of Odysseus to visit many cities and people and to attain

[26] *Met.* III. 26, IV. 6.   [27] *Met.* IX. 30.
[28] *Met.* VII. 10–12.   [29] *Met.* VII. 2–3.

knowledge and wisdom.[30] He is aware, as he utters
diatribes against the corruption of lawyers and judges,
that someone will exclaim : "Really ! Shall we now permit an ass to philosophize for us ?"[31] Finally in the last
book,[32] before the description of his own initiation, he
addresses the reader as *studiose,* declares that perhaps
now the reader is excited by a religious longing and ex-
pects him to hear and believe the truth as Lucius reveals
his ecstatic experience in initiation. Through these various appeals to the reader there is suggested a subtle
change in his assumed attitude. First the reader is to be
entertained. Then the story is to be made plausible to
him. Next his curiosity about life and men is to be
gratified. And though he may resent the ass's philosophizing, he is finally carried along with Lucius in an intense desire to know the truth about a religious experience which will set him free.

The general patterns of the stories have already been
referred to in the accounts of them. They divide into
simple, progressive narratives, groups of stories in sequence, and convoluted story within story within story
for contrast or emphasis. Within these rather simple
plans, multiplex and varied devices are used for gaining
effects.

There is no monotony in the settings of the stories.
The reader is transported to bedroom in inn, dinner
party in palace, court-room, house of miser, hut of poor
old baggage, elegant palace, robbers' mountain fastness,
a baker's mill, a rich tyrant's farm. In the story of
Charite the scene shifts from her home to the forest where
the boar hunt takes place, from her bedroom where she
puts out the eyes of Thrasyllus to the sepulchre of her
husband where she kills herself. In the story of Cupid

[30] *Met.* IX. 13–15.　　　[31] *Met.* X. 33.　　　[32] *Met.* XI. 23.

and Psyche with almost cinematic shifting we behold the
house of her parents, the lonely mountain top, the palace
of Cupid, Venus' golden bedroom, the temples of Ceres
and of Juno, the royal palace of Jupiter, the lower world,
Olympus with all its glorious assemblage of gods.   Part
of the brilliancy of the narrative consists in many a *pur-
pureus pannus* of vivid description of some special scene :
the robbers' cave, Byrrhaena's house, Cupid's palace, the
baker's mill, and in these pictures realistic details develop
the atmosphere desired of horror, of beauty, or of pathos.

Even more varied than the settings of the stories are
the characters who pass swiftly before our eyes in this
pageant of adventure.   With Lucius, man or ass, always
leading the procession, advance witches, miser, pompous
aedile, wanton maid, elegant matron, Chaldean charla-
tan, thaumaturgic Egyptian, bandits with brave chieftains, terrified old cook, kidnaped bride, gallant husband, false lover, phantom ghosts, poor shepherds with
their flocks and dogs, cruel masters, rich tyrants, wanton
wives, deceived husbands, cunning lovers, murderesses
and corrupt slaves, venal physician and upright physician, lewd Syrian priests, rapt Egyptian priests, bright
Olympian deities made in the image of man, and last of
all the mystic figure of Isis, goddess of many-names, goddess of salvation.   No chance for boredom is afforded the
reader in this great cinema of innumerable scenes and
characters.

And the cinema is a talking movie, rich in conversations and speeches.   A character that has been given no
name and has seemed a mere type speaks and is revealed
no automaton but a human being whom we understand
from his words.   Turn the pages of the *Metamorphoses*
rapidly as though it were a novel of today and you will
see how much conversation and direct speech enlivens the

narrative. One story may be taken to illustrate the variety in their use.

The first *novella*, Socrates and the witch Meroe,[33] is set with a prologue and epilogue of discussion about its credibility by the fellow-travelers of the narrator. The plight of Socrates in the toils of his witch mistress is revealed by the conversation between himself and Aristomenes. The atmosphere of horror and fear is set by the long description which Socrates gives to his friend of Meroe's powers. The main event, the murder of Socrates, is accompanied by the chatter of the foul old beldames. Aristomenes' terror after their departure is expressed in soliloquy. The plot develops in his attempt to escape through his argument with the drowsy ostler. Failing in that plan, Aristomenes apostrophizes his bed and begs it for a rope to hang himself. The unexpected awakening of Socrates starts a lively narrative of their nightmares by the two friends to each other. The ultimate fatality of Socrates' death is brought about by a single sentence of advice from his friend to quench his thirst by a drink from the flowing stream. It is clear that this story depends almost entirely on direct speech and conversation for its development.

Throughout the novel one of Apuleius' most effective methods is this varied use of conversation and speeches. Sometimes a simple short question reveals the point of the whole story. "In this place are dead men wont to run away?" [34] Again a long speech with cumulative effect sets the atmosphere of the tale as when Socrates describes at length the powers of the witch, Meroe.[35] Characters are effectively painted by their own words : for example, the wicked sisters of Psyche reveal in conversation their jealousy, venality and cruelty.[36] Certain

[33] *Met.* I. 5-20.　　[34] *Met.* II. 21.　　[35] *Met.* I. 8-10.　　[36] *Met.* V. 9-10.

speeches highly colored by emotion advance plot or form
climax. When the outraged Venus angrily upbraids
Cupid, we see that Psyche has made a dangerous enemy
who will torture her with long suffering.[37]   The impassioned denunciation by Charite of the sleeping Thrasyllus prepares us for her act of vengeance and her suicide.[38]
The short speech of the amorous stepmother to the grave
young hero lays the corner-stone of this tragedy.[39]   In
the eleventh book, the inner meaning of the worship of
Isis is developed by the ardent prayers of Lucius,[40] by
the mystic revelation in long speech of the goddess herself,[41] and by the consolation of her priest's great benediction for the hero, her new follower.[42]

These few illustrations serve to suggest Apuleius'
skillful art.   In stories short and long on rather simple
general outlines he shows the practiced technique of the
great story-teller by his skillful use of different narrators
and audiences, of various settings and detailed descriptions, of a multitude of vital persons whose own natural
words portray their characters and tell their stories.   And
that exotic Latin for which he apologized with its prodi-
gious vocabulary, its compelling melodies, its peculiar
contrasts, its sudden simplicities, clothes the novel in very
rococo garments that suit its picaresque corporality.

This study of the *novelle* in Apuleius' novel and his
art in telling them has prepared the way for a review of
his general themes and for reflections on their inter-relations.   Adventure is primarily his concern whether it be
the adventure of the open road that leads from city to city
or an inner pilgrim's progress up the hill of doubt to the
City of God.   The plot is not solved until after many
wanderings the ass is retransformed to human shape, of

37 *Met.* V. 29–30.   38 *Met.* VIII. 12.   39 *Met.* X. 3.
40 *Met.* XI. 2 ; XI. 25.   41 *Met.* XI. 4–6.   42 *Met.* XI. 15.

almost divine aspects. Lucius' greatest adventure is his own double metamorphosis.

These most important events of his life open up worlds of other experiences as his fortunes transfer him from one owner to another, from city to city, with group after group of companions, witches, magicians, robbers, shepherds, tyrants, priests, soldiers, rich man, poor man, baker, smith, fuller, women leal and faithless, outraged husbands and cunning adulterers, until he says good-bye to all that and is absorbed in a mystic adventure that transcends all earthly experiences. For Lucius man or ass must have his excitement ; life is never to be dull for one whose curiosity keeps him constantly journeying on earth and sending his soul to the invisible in search of heaven.

A rich humanity colors his record of adventures and part of the high art of having a man-ass the narrator of the story consisted in the *rapport* which this change gave him with beasts as well as men. For Lucius is full of sympathy for maltreated animals as well as for the oppressed poor, and by a hundred small details makes the reader see their pitiful sufferings and weary labor. The misuse of power is horrible to him whether an *instans tyrannus* tortures a servant and a rich man robs a poor neighbor, or whether relentless drivers beat and goad overburdened beasts. The hard life of the humble finds a new expression in these pages.

Sex is no less prominent than in modern novels and is treated openly. It is noticeable that the *cinaedus* motif plays here a very minor part in contrast to its predominant use in the *Satyricon*. It forms the climax of the story of the fuller's wife and colors the whole description of the Syrian priests, but their lewdness is viewed by the ass with complete horror.

Women are depicted in their relation to men in two types, wanton and faithful, so that what we might call the Fotis motif (wantonness of servant or wife) and the Charite motif (pure devotion) keep recurring through the stories. The realistic description of the amorous Fotis in the first book is a motivation of the later Milesian Tales of faithless wives. The long love-story of Charite in the center of the novel has for a companion piece the sublimated Milesian Tale of Psyche, the soul of woman, who is always true to her first love through all her trials. The Cupid-Psyche story with its vague symbolism forecasts a change from the adventures of sex to the experiences of mystic religion which finally saves Lucius' soul.

For to the thoughtful reader it must be evident that through all the adventures of this novel the hero is in quest of a permanent satisfaction. He is ever eager to penetrate beyond the visible and the tangible to phenomena less evident but more vital. So first he pursues magic art, gathers information, experiments disastrously. Yet in the long period of his transformation he becomes intuitively aware of strange identities in nature of man and beast and enters vicariously into the lives of both. This identification of himself with a four-footed creature serves to open a world of folk-lore to him and brings him through old *märchen* into a fairy realm of chanting waters, serving winds, gossiping gull, friendly ants, musical reed. And in that world echoes of a far-off dimly remembered Platonism come to him so that he thinks of Amor and Psyche as bright youths in love, one god, one mortal, surrounded by deities. And through these strange glasses of folk-lore and Platonic philosophy the Olympian hierarchy is seen in a new Lucianic light as part of a brilliant story, wherein the great gods are very near man in form and character.

But the old story fails to satisfy, and the hero must struggle on, viewing every corruption of religion, of family life, of social life, until at last he is forced to be a part of these horrors and must submit in ass's shape to obscene degradation in public spectacle. Then his own horrified revolt effects his escape and through prayer, vision, ecstasy and benediction he is saved and restored to human shape by Isis, and her mystic cult. If Lucius is not meant to be Everyman or Everyass at least he conveys to every reader the sense of universal experience, the homo facing fundamental concepts of mind and matter, of body and soul, of sex and religion, of subconscious and superconscious forces in conflict for or in his life. The significant conclusion of the novel in the startling eleventh book is the experience of mystic ecstasy, by revelation, conversion and adoration. Lucius descends to hell and ascends into heaven, wanders through all the elements, meets the gods face to face, finally becomes the worshiper and lover of the goddess Isis forever. The central story of the novel, the love-story of Cupid and Psyche, in which Psyche is made immortal seems to forecast this story of conversion in which man is transformed into votary worthy of his divine Lady and worshiped by the people as a god himself.

Perhaps I may seem to have overemphasized a theme of spiritual quest and growth in Apuleius' novel but for me it is there, now vaguely hinted, now clearly developed. May it not be significant that when Apuleius is converted he no longer goes four-footed but again rides his white horse, Candidus, strangely restored to him? Certainly the central position in the novel of the Cupid and Psyche story with its suggestions of hidden meaning makes it more than a fairy-story or a love-story. And the solemn nature of the long final book with its impressive pageantry, visions, prayers, conversion, exaltation, benedictions, must convince any reader that at the end Lucius the votary of Isis is a far different person from the Lucius of the first book, the curious traveler in Thessaly, land of magic.

The very art of Apuleius conceals in the rich overlay of stories this change in his hero's point of view and nature. Anyone who reads the *Apologia,* the speech of self-defense which Apuleius made in his trial for the use of magic, must be convinced that the writer was a sophisticated artist who calculated and understood his effects on hearers or readers. And his *Florida* confirms this belief. In his novel I think that Apuleius was working out the besetting problems of his age and his relation to them, not by deep thinking or systematic philosophy but pragmatically through adventure, experience and reflection. The *Metamorphoses* seems to me indeed, as Lucius himself hinted, a veritable Odyssey of the life of an extraordinary hero in the age of the Antonines.

BIBLIOGRAPHY

I. GENERAL WORKS ON GREEK AND LATIN LITERATURE INCLUDING ANCIENT FICTION

Butler, H. E., *Post-Augustan Poetry from Seneca to Juvenal.* Oxford, 1909.

Calderini, A., *Il Pensiero greco*, vol. 8. *Caritone di Afrodisia : Le Avventure di Cherea e Calliroe.* Milano — Roma, 1913.

Chassang, A., *Les Romans grecs.* Paris, 1880.

Chauvin, V., *Les Romanciers grecs et latins.* Paris, 1864.

Crump, M. M., *The Epyllion from Theocritus to Ovid.* Oxford, 1931.

Dill, Samuel, *Roman Society from Nero to Marcus Aurelius.* London, 1911.

Duff, J. Wight, *A Literary History of Rome from the Origins to the Close of the Golden Age.* New York, 1927.

———, *A Literary History of Rome in the Silver Age from Tiberius to Hadrian.* New York, 1927.

Dunlop, John, *History of Fiction.* 2 vols. Philadelphia, 1842.

Fowler, W. Warde, *Social Life at Rome in the Age of Cicero.* London, 1922.

Glover, T. R., *Life and Letters in the Fourth Century.* Cambridge, 1901.

Hardie, W. R., *Lectures on Classical Subjects.* London, 1903.

Lavagnini, B., *Le Origini del Romanzo greco.* Pisa, 1921.

Mackail, J. W., *Latin Literature.* New York, 1923.

———, *Lectures on Greek Poetry.* New York, 1910.

———, *Lectures on Poetry.* New York, 1911.

Murray, Gilbert, *A History of Ancient Greek Literature.* New York, 1935.

Phillimore, J. S., "Greek Romances," in *English Literature and the Classics.* Oxford, 1912.

Rattenbury, R. M., "Romance : Traces of Lost Greek Novels," in *New Chapters in the History of Greek Literature, Third Series.* Oxford, 1933.

Rohde, Erwin, *Der griechische Roman und seine Vorläufer.* Leipzig, 1914.

Summers, W. C., *The Silver Age of Latin Literature from Tiberius to Trajan.* New York, 1920.

Teuffel, W. S., and Schwabe, L., *History of Roman Literature,* translated by G. C. W. Warr. 2 vols. London, 1900.

II. ORIENTAL STORIES IN CLASSICAL PROSE LITERATURE

Andrae, A., "Sophonisbe in der französischen Tragödie mit Berucksichtigung der Sophonisbebearbeitungen in anderen Literaturen," in *Zeitschrift für Neufranzösische Sprache und Litteratur,* 2–10, Supp. 6, 1891.

Godley, A. D., *Herodotus,* Translation with Greek text, in *The Loeb Classical Library.* 4 vols. New York, 1921–1924.

Miller, Walter, *Cyropaedia* by Xenophon, Translation with Greek text, in *The Loeb Classical Library.* 2 vols. New York, 1914.

Rogers, B. B., *Aristophanes,* Translation with Greek text, in *The Loeb Classical Library.* 3 vols. New York, 1930.

Taine, H., *Essai sur Tite Live.* Paris, 1904.

Thomson, J. A. K., *The Art of the Logos.* London, 1935.

———, *Irony : An Historical Introduction.* London, 1926.

Thornley, G., and Edmonds, J. M., *Daphnis and Chloe,* by Longus, Translation with Greek text ; Gaselee, S., *The Love Romances of Parthenius,* Translation with Greek text, in *The Loeb Classical Library.* New York, 1924.

III. LITTLE STORIES IN LATIN ELEGIAC INSCRIPTIONS

Corpus Inscriptionum Graecarum, XIV. Berolini apud G. Reimerum, 1890.

Corpus Inscriptionum Latinarum. Berolini apud G. Reimerum, 1863–1931.

Abbott, F. F., *Society and Politics in Ancient Rome.* New York, 1909.

Buecheler, F., *Anthologia Latina, Carmina Latina Epigraphica,* vols. II 1, 2, III supplementum. Leipzig, 1895, 1897, 1926.

Cagnat, R., "Sur les Manuels professionels des Graveurs d'Inscriptions romaines," in *Rev. de Phil.,* vol. XIII (1889).

della Corte, M., *Pompeii, the New Excavations.* Valle di Pompei, 1925.

Galletier, Edouard, *Étude sur la Poésie funéraire romaine d'après les Inscriptions. Thèse présentée a la Faculté des Lettres de Paris.* Paris, 1922.

Lier, Bruno, "Topica carminum sepulcralium latinorum," in
Philologus, vol. LXII (1903) and vol. LXIII (1904).
Mair, A. W., *Callimachus and Lycophron*, Mair, G. R., *Aratus*,
Translation with Greek text, in *The Loeb Classical Library*.
New York, 1921.
Mau, August, *Pompeii, its Life and Art*, translated by Francis
W. Kelsey. New York, 1907.
Paton, W. R., *The Greek Anthology*, Translation with Greek
text, in *The Loeb Classical Library*. 5 vols. New York,
1916-1918.
Plessis, Frédéric, *Poésie latine Epitaphes*. Paris, 1905.

IV. SATIRE AND THE LATIN NOVEL

Abbott, F. F., *The Common People of Ancient Rome*. New
York, 1920.
Ball, A. P., *The Satire of Seneca on the Apotheosis of Claudius*.
New York, 1902.
Boissier, Gaston, *L'Opposition sous les Césars*. Paris, 1928.
Buecheler, F., *Petronii saturae et liber Priapeorum ; adiectae sunt
Varronis et Senecae saturae similesque reliquiae*. Berlin,
1904.
Collignon, A., *Étude sur Pétrone*. Paris, 1892.
Fowler, H. W., and Fowler, F. G., *The Works of Lucian of
Samosata*, (translation). 4 vols. Oxford, 1905.
Hadas, M., "Oriental Elements in Petronius," in *American
Journal of Philology*, vol. L (1929).
Harmon, A. M., *Lucian*, Translation with Greek text, in *The
Loeb Classical Library*. 8 vols. New York, 1913-1925.
Helm, R., *Lucian und Menipp*. Leipzig, 1906.
Heseltine, M., *Petronius*, Translation with Latin text ; Rouse,
W. H. D., *Seneca Apocolocyntosis*, Translation with Latin
text, in *The Loeb Classical Library*. New York, 1930.
Hicks, R. D., *Diogenes Laertius, Lives of Eminent Philosophers*,
Translation with Greek text, in *The Loeb Classical Library*.
2 vols. New York, 1925.
Livingstone, R. W., *The Mission of Greece*. Oxford, 1928.
Martha, C., *Les Moralistes sous l'Empire romain*. Paris, 1894.
Marx, F., *C. Lucilii Carminum Reliquiae*. 2 vols. Leipzig,
1904-1905.
Mendell, C. W., "Petronius and the Greek Romance," in *Classical Philology*, vol. XII (1917).
Merry, W. W., *Selected Fragments of Roman Poetry*. Oxford,
1891.

Mommsen, T., *The History of Rome*, translated by William P. Dickson. 4 vols. New York, 1887.

Peck, H. T., *Trimalchio's Dinner by Petronius Arbiter*. New York, 1898.

Rolfe, J. C., *Suetonius*, Translation with Latin text, in *The Loeb Classical Library*. 2 vols. New York, 1914.

Perry, B. E., "Petronius and the Comic Romance," in *Classical Philology*, vol. XX (1925).

Shero, L. R., "The *Cena* in Roman Satire," in *Classical Philology*, vol. XVIII (1923).

Thomas, Émile, *Pétrone*. Paris, 1902.

Tiddy, R. J. E., "Satura and Satire," in *English Literature and the Classics*. Oxford, 1912.

Terzaghi, N., *Per la Storia della Satira*. Torino, 1932.

V. Prose Fiction in the Augustan Age : Seneca's Controversiae

Boissier, G., *Tacitus and other Roman Studies*, translated by W. G. Hutchison. London, 1906.

Bornecque, H., *Sénèque le Rhéteur : Controverses et Suasoires*. 2 vols. Paris, 1932.

Butler, H. E., *Institutio Oratoria of Quintilian*, Translation with Latin text, in *The Loeb Classical Library*. 4 vols. New York, 1921–1922.

Edward, W. A., *The Suasoriae of Seneca the Elder*. Cambridge, 1928.

Friedländer, L., *Roman Life and Manners under the Early Empire*, translated by J. H. Freese. 4 vols. New York, 1913.

Lehnert, G., *Quintiliani quae feruntur Declamationes XIX Maiores*. Leipzig, 1905.

Morawski, K. v., "Zu lateinischen Schriftstellern," in *Wiener Studien*, vol. IV (1882).

Perry, B. E., "On Apuleius' *Metamorphoses* II, 31 – III, 20," in *American Journal of Philology*, vol. XLVI (1925).

Ramsay, G. G., *Juvenal and Persius*, Translation with Latin text in *The Loeb Classical Library*. New York, 1924.

Ritter, C., *M. Fabii Quintiliani Declamationes quae supersunt CXLV*. Leipzig, 1884.

Robertson, D. S., "A Greek Carnival," in *Journal of Hellenic Studies*, vol. XXXIX (1919).

Simonds, T. S., *The Themes Treated by the Elder Seneca*. (Dissertation). Baltimore, 1896.

VI. Apuleius' Art of Story-Telling
Editions and Translations into English

Adlington, W., (1566) revised by Gaselee, S., *Apuleius: The Golden Ass*, Translation with Latin text, in *The Loeb Classical Library*. New York, 1915.

Butler, H. E., *The Apologia and Florida*, 1909 ; *The Metamorphoses*. 2 vols. 1910, (translation), Oxford.

——, and Owen, A. S., (editors), *Apologia*. Oxford, 1914.

Helm, R., (editor), *Apulei opera quae supersunt*. Leipzig, 1912, 1913, 1921.

Oudendorp, F. van, and Hildebrand, G. F., (editors), *L. Apulei opera omnia*. Leipzig, 1842.

Purser, L. C., (editor), *The Story of Cupid and Psyche as related by Apuleius*. London, 1910.

Stuttaford, Charles, *Apuleius: The Story of Cupid and Psyche*, (translation). London, 1903.

Articles and Books on Apuleius

Abt, A., *Die Apologie des Apuleius von Madaura und die antike Zauberei*. Giessen, 1907.

Cocchia, E., *Romanzo e Realtà nella Vita — e nell' Attività letteraria di Lucio Apuleio*. Catania, 1915.

de Jong, K. H. E., *De Apuleio isiacorum mysteriorum teste*. (Dissertation). Leyden, 1900.

Monceaux, Paul, *Apulée. Roman et Magie*. Paris, 1888.

Norden, Fritz, *Apulejus von Madaura und das römische Privatrecht*. Leipzig, 1912.

Oldfather, W. A., Canter, H. V., Perry, B. E., *Index Apuleianus* in *Philological Monographs* published by the American Philological Association, number III. Middletown, Connecticut, 1934.

Perry, B. E., *The Metamorphoses ascribed to Lucius of Patrae*. (Princeton University Dissertation). Lancaster, Pa., 1920.

——, "An Interpretation of Apuleius' *Metamorphoses*," in T. P. A. P. A., vol. LVII (1926).

——, "On the Authenticity of *Lucius sive asinus*," in *Classical Philology*, vol. XXI (1926).

——, "Some Aspects of the Literary Art of Apuleius," in T. P. A. P. A., vol. LIV (1923).

For further Bibliography see Haight, E. H., *Apuleius and his Influence* in *Our Debt to Greece and Rome*. New York, 1927.

INDEX

201